guide to Gettysburg Battlefield Monuments

guide to **Gettysburg Battlefield Monuments**

monument descriptions by Tom Huntington

STACKPOLE
BOOKS

Published by
STACKPOLE BOOKS
5067 Ritter Road
Mechanicsburg, PA 17055
www.stackpolebooks.com

Printed in the United States of America

10 9 8 7 6 5 4 3 2 1

First edition

Photographs by Tom Huntington and Mark Allison
Cover design by Caroline M. Stover

Library of Congress Cataloging-in-Publication Data

Huntington, Tom, 1960–
  Guide to Gettysburg battlefield monuments / monument descriptions by Tom Huntington. — First edition.
    pages cm
  ISBN 978-0-8117-1233-0
  1. Battlefield monuments—Pennsylvania—Gettysburg National Military Park—Guidebooks. 2. Gettysburg National Military Park (Pa.)—Guidebooks. 3. Pennsylvania—History—Civil War, 1861–1865—Monuments—Guidebooks. 4. United States—History—Civil War, 1861–1865—Monuments—Guidebooks. 5. Gettysburg, Battle of, Gettysburg, Pa., 1863. I. Title.
  E475.56.H86 2013
  973.7'349—dc23
                                                    2012051205

CONTENTS

ABOUT THIS GUIDE

This guide allows you to locate every monument and tablet on the Gettysburg Battlefield. It also tells you a bit about each monument, the division or person each one honors, and what the honoree did during the fighting. It is intended to be carried along during a visit to Gettysburg; it can also, of course, be studied at home.

There are 466 monuments and 367 tablets in the Gettysburg National Military Park, which encompasses some nine square miles. This guide includes photos, descriptions, map locations, and GPS coordinates of all the monuments. It includes listings, locations, and coordinates for all the tablets.

The monument descriptions and photos are organized by state, since most monuments honor specific regiments from a particular state. Monuments that memorialize brigades, divisions, people, or the entire Union or Confederate army follow the state monuments. Each description includes a reference to one of the guide's maps, GPS coordinates, and the year of the monument's dedication.

The battlefield's tablets themselves feature text that pertains to a specific unit's activities during the battle. In this guide, tablet lists are arranged by state, unit, person, or army, as appropriate. Like the monument descriptions, each tablet listing includes GPS coordinates and a map reference.

SUMMARY OF THE BATTLE

JULY 1: FIRST DAY

Early on July 1, 1863, a relatively small number of Union and Confederate soldiers clashed along the Chambersburg Pike, just northwest of Gettysburg, Pennsylvania. The fighting intensified throughout the day as both sides moved distant troops to the field—Confederates coming from the west and north and the Union arriving from the south. By nightfall, Union troops were driven back through town. They halted their retreat on Cemetery Hill.

JULY 2: SECOND DAY

Union troops, now reinforced, positioned themselves in a curving defensive line that extended from Culp's Hill west to Cemetery Hill and south along Cemetery Ridge toward Little Round Top. In the afternoon, Confederate forces attacked both the Union right and left. Fierce fighting—up Culp's Hill and on Little Round Top, at Devil's Den, in the Wheatfield, and through the Peach Orchard—killed and wounded large numbers of men on both sides, but the federal position was left much the same as it was at the start of the day.

JULY 3: THIRD DAY

Following an early-morning attack on the Union right, the Confederates unleashed a massive artillery bombardment to soften the Union center. At around two in the afternoon, three Confederate divisions (one led by Gen. George Pickett) charged a mile through open fields toward federal positions on Cemetery Ridge. By then, the fighting on the right had ended, and even though rebel forces managed to breach the Union line at several spots, the Confederates were quickly driven back. They quit the field completely during the night, heading to Virginia in retreat.

Some 833 monuments and tablets honor the troops who fought the Battle of Gettysburg.

MONUMENT DESCRIPTIONS

ALABAMA

819. 4th Alabama Infantry

The 4th Alabama was part of Evander Law's brigade of Hood's division, and it moved out to attack the Union left from around this spot on July 2, with "charges of canister passing over us with the noise of partridges in flight," as one soldier recalled. This marker was the first (and only) monument the War Department created for a Confederate regiment when it administered the park.

Dedicated in 1904
39.787214, -77.254056; see map EE

822. Alabama State Monument

Alabama seceded from the Union on January 11, 1861. Its capital, Montgomery, hosted the convention that created the Confederate States of America, and Montgomery became the CSA's first capital. As many as 125,000 Alabamians fought for the Confederacy during the war. Dedicated on November 12, 1933, the state's monument stands near the spot where Evander Law's Alabama brigade moved out to attack the Union left flank on July 2.

Dedicated in 1933
39.78669, -77.254153; see map EE

5

ARKANSAS

667. Arkansas State Monument

When President Lincoln requested soldiers to put down the rebellion, Arkansas governor Henry M. Rector replied that the state would fight against "Northern mendacity and usurpation." Arkansas seceded from the Union on May 6, 1861. In the latter stages of the war, the state had two governments, one pro-Southern and one pro-Northern. Some soldiers from Arkansas fought for the Union.

Dedicated in 1966
39.79262, -77.255159; see map AA

CONNECTICUT

617. 2nd Battery, Connecticut Artillery (Sterling's Battery)

Also known as Sterling's Battery, the 2nd Battery of the Connecticut Light Artillery posted its weapons on this spot along the Union artillery line on July 3. The battery was a green unit that had gotten its first real taste of combat on July 2.

Dedicated in 1889
39.803723, -77.234509; see map W

362. 5th Connecticut Infantry

The 5th Connecticut fought at Gettysburg under the command of Col. Warren W. Packer. "It was our good fortune that, though sent to almost every part of the line as emergency required, the regiment was not seriously engaged, and our losses were light," said Lt. Col. John B. Lewis, the regimental surgeon, when this "chaste and beautiful monument" was dedicated in 1887.

Dedicated in 1887
39.815579, -77.217408; see map O

218. 14th Connecticut Infantry

One of the few infantry regiments armed with the Sharps breech-loading rifle, the 14th Connecticut captured the farm buildings of William Bliss, which had been sheltering Confederate sharpshooters, on the morning of July 3. A position marker stands at the site.

Dedicated in 1884
39.813815, -77.235415; see map M

197. 14th Connecticut Infantry

The buildings of William and Adeline Bliss provided shelter for Confederate sharpshooters. On July 3, several Union regiments, including the 14th Connecticut, moved forward, drove the rebels from the farm, and set fire to the buildings. The regiment's main monument is on Hancock Avenue.

39.816375, -77.242027; see map M

66. 17th Connecticut Infantry

The 17th Connecticut was commanded by Lt. Col. Douglas Fowler, who insisted on remaining on horseback. "Dodge the big ones, boys," Fowler joked to his men as enemy shells flew toward them. After ordering his men to charge, Fowler was killed by a bullet to the head. The regiment has another monument on Wainwright Avenue.

Dedicated in 1903
39.845459, -77.226195; see map D

223. 17ᵗʰ Connecticut Infantry

On the evening of July 2, the 17ᵗʰ Connecticut engaged in a furious defense against the onrushing brigade of Harry Hays's Louisiana Tigers from Jubal Early's division. "We had a hand-to-hand conflict with them, firmly held our ground, and drove them back," reported Maj. Allen G. Brady.

Dedicated in 1886–1893
39.82262, -77.22816; see map N

359. 20ᵗʰ Connecticut Infantry

Sent early on July 3 to retake fortifications at the base of Culp's Hill, the 20ᵗʰ Connecticut advanced under the cover of artillery, "fighting as best we could, shielding ourselves behind rocks & trees," recalled the regiment's commander, Lt. Col. William Wooster. Low on ammunition, the regiment was relieved by the 123ʳᵈ New York.

Dedicated in 1885
39.815776, -77.217789; see map O

720. 27ᵗʰ Connecticut Infantry

Part of the 2ⁿᵈ Corps, the 27ᵗʰ Connecticut hurried to the Wheatfield to support the collapsing 3ʳᵈ Corps, Lt. Col. Henry Merwin in command. "Merwin falls while leading the command with his accustomed bravery," read a regimental history. "The contest at this point continued for some time. Planting the colors upon the top, the men loaded their pieces under shelter of the brow of the hill, then, rising up, delivered their fire." Merwin has a small marker on Wheatfield Road.

Dedicated in 1889
39.797077, -77.241624; see map BB

714. 27th Connecticut Infantry

The 27th Connecticut's main monument is in the Wheatfield. On July 2, they pushed the enemy out of the Wheatfield and into the woods beyond, where they were hit with "a withering fire." After some time, the federals were in turn pushed back through the Wheatfield.

Dedicated in 1885
39.795373, -77.24711; see map BB

DELAWARE

214. 1st Delaware Infantry

The 1st Delaware Infantry battled for the Bliss farm buildings on July 2 (a small marker indicates their location) and resisted the Confederate charge of July 3 on this spot. Lt. William Smith was in command during the fighting. "He was a brave and efficient officer, and was instantly killed, with one of the enemy's captured flags in his hand," reported the brigade commander, Col. Thomas Smyth. "When picked up, his sword was found in one hand and a catured rebel flag in the other," recounted a history.

Dedicated in 1886–1893
39.814576, -77.235469; see map M

194. 1st Delaware Infantry

The 1st Delaware was one of the regiments ordered forward to this spot to drive Confederate sharpshooters from the Bliss farm buildings on July 3. The regiment's main monument is on Hancock Avenue.

39.817086, -77.241643; see map M

718. 2nd Delaware Infantry

The 2nd Delaware, part of Caldwell's division of the 2nd Corps, fought through the Wheatfield and into the Rose Woods when the division was sent to aid the 3rd Corps on July 2. After pushing the rebels into the trees, the Union soldiers were forced to withdraw. "In this engagement our loss was severe," reported Col. William P. Baily.

Dedicated in 1885
39.794759, -77.247137; see map BB

211. 2nd Delaware Infantry

This small position marker indicates the position of the 2nd Delaware Infantry on July 3 when it participated in the repulse of Pickett's Charge.

39.81479, -77.235496; see map M

290. Delaware State Monument

Delaware was a slave-holding state when war broke out in 1861, but it remained loyal to the Union. About 12,000 soldiers from Delaware served in the federal forces. The 1st and 2nd Delaware fought at Gettysburg, and three of their soldiers earned the Medal of Honor here. The bas-relief by sculptor Ron Tunison depicts the 1st and 2nd Delaware following the repulse of Pickett's Charge. Tunison used his own face on a surrendering Southerner.

Dedicated in 2000
39.816099, -77.232538; see map N

> *"For three days the tumult and roar around Cemetery Heights and the Round Tops seemed the echo of the internal commotion which ages before had heaved these hills above the surrounding plain."*
>
> —Confederate Brig. Gen. John B. Gordon

FLORIDA

432. Florida State Monument

Florida seceded from the United States on January 10, 1861, the third state to do so. Three regiments fought in Gen. E. A. Perry's Florida Brigade of Richard Anderson's division in the Army of Northern Virginia's 3rd Corps at Gettysburg. "They were hotly engaged," reported Anderson, "and did not retire until compelled, like all the others, to do so by the superior force of the enemy, and the great strength of his position."

Dedicated in 1963
39.810214, -77.254142; see map U

GEORGIA

654. Georgia State Monument

Georgia seceded from the Union on January 19, 1861, giving the Confederacy a territory that extended uninterrupted to the Mississippi River. During the war Georgia provided some 100,000 soldiers to the rebellion. The monument was dedicated in September 1961; that month an identical monument was also dedicated on the Antietam Battlefield.

Dedicated in 1961
39.798859, -77.255979; see map AA

ILLINOIS

1. 1st Shot Marker (Company E, 8th Illinois Cavalry)

Around 7:30 on the morning of July 1, Lt. Marcellus Jones of the 8th Illinois Cavalry's Company E borrowed a Sharps carbine, steadied it on a rail fence, and fired at approaching Confederate soldiers. It was the first shot of the Battle of Gettysburg (although members of the 9th New York Cavalry disputed the 8th Illinois' claim).

Dedicated in 1883
39.850921, -77.280727; see map A

79. 8th Illinois Cavalry

Following its initial clash with the advancing rebels on the Chambersburg Pike, the 8th Illinois Cavalry fought a delaying action as it retreated here. Pvt. David Diffenbaugh, whose name is on the monument, was the regiment's only fatality at Gettysburg. He died while on duty at the brigade's headquarters.

Dedicated in 1891
39.850921, -77.280727; see map G

107. 12th Illinois Cavalry

The 12th Illinois Cavalry established its line of battle here on July 1 but was "compelled to give slowly back before superior numbers of the enemy," said brigade commander George H. Chapman. The saddle on top of the marker is an obvious indication of this regiment's branch of the army.

Dedicated in 1891
39.837051, -77.248504; see map G

52. 82nd Illinois Infantry

The commander of the 82nd Illinois, Lt. Col. Edward Salomon, reported that he led his regiment and the 61st Ohio into Gettysburg during the retreat on July 1; they were the last Union regiments to reach town. Salomon's horse was killed and fell on top of him, but soldiers managed to help the injured officer to Cemetery Hill.

Dedicated in 1891
39.842811, -77.232333; see map C

INDIANA

103. 3rd Indiana Cavalry

This cavalry regiment fought under the command of Col. George H. Chapman, who also commanded the 1st Brigade of the 1st Cavalry Division. The arriving Confederates pushed the cavalry slowly back on July 1. "We did not relinquish the position, however, until relieved by the advance of the 1st Army Corps," reported Chapman.

Dedicated in 1885
39.837906, -77.247906; see map G

318. 7th Indiana Infantry

On his own initiative, Col. Ira Grover took the 7th Indiana from its rearguard position and marched toward the sound of the guns, reaching this position on Culp's Hill just in time to interrupt a Confederate attempt to capture it.

Dedicated in 1885
39.820292, -77.220442; see map O

243. 14th Indiana Infantry

The 14th Indiana was part of Samuel Carroll's brigade in the 2nd Corps. On the night of July 2, it rushed forward to defend East Cemetery Hill's Union batteries from Jubal Early's Confederates. "We charged past the battery while they fired over us, and we drove the rebels with great loss," noted Lt. Col. Elijah H. C. Cavins. "Our fight lasted only a few minutes, but was desperate."

39.821494, -77.228951; see map N

96. 19th Indiana Infantry

The 19th Indiana, part of the Iron Brigade, reached here on July 1 and prepared to meet the advancing Confederates of Archer's brigade. "The charge was made with great spirit and celerity," noted Col. Samuel Williams in his report. In the afternoon, outflanked on the left, the regiment withdrew to Seminary Ridge and then to Cemetery Hill.

Dedicated in 1885
39.834184, -77.254331; see map G

749. 20th Indiana Infantry

On July 2, the 20th Indiana moved forward on the right of its brigade and met the enemy around 4:00 pm. "The brigade soon after advanced to the brow of a small hill, about 150 yards from the position it occupied when first attacked," reported Lt. Col. William C. L. Taylor, who had assumed command after the death of Col. John Wheeler. The regiment retired with the rest of the brigade.

Dedicated in 1885
39.794806, -77.242834; see map BB

374. 27th Indiana Infantry

The 27th Indiana's colonel was Silas Colgrove (for whom Colgrove Avenue was named) until he was promoted to brigade command. On July 3, this regiment and the 2nd Massachusetts attempted to drive the rebels from Union defenses they had occupied. Instead of sending skirmishers first, Colgrove sent out both regiments, which were driven back. Division commander Thomas Ruger decided "it was one of those unfortunate occurrences that will happen in the excitement of battle."

Dedicated in 1885
39.813577, -77.215989; see map O

373. 27th Indiana Infantry

This marker indicates the farthest advance of the 27th Indiana on July 3. "It became evident to me that scarcely a man could live to gain the position of the enemy," reported brigade commander Silas Colgrove. "I ordered the regiment to fall back behind its breastworks, which it did." The regiment's main monument is nearby on Colgrove Avenue.

39.814353, -77.216055; see map O

372. State of Indiana Monument

Erected in 1970, Indiana's monument commemorates a state that contributed more than 61,000 soldiers to the Union cause. Five Hoosier infantry regiments fought at Gettysburg, plus units from two cavalry regiments.

Dedicated in 1970
39.814184, -77.21631; see map O

KENTUCKY

267. Kentucky Monument

As a border state, Kentucky sent soldiers to both the Union (76,000) and the Confederacy (25,000). President Abraham Lincoln and Confederate president Jefferson Davis were both born in Kentucky, but the Kentucky Memorial chooses to honor Lincoln by quoting his Gettysburg Address, which the president delivered at a spot somewhere between the monument and the Evergreen Cemetery fence.

Dedicated on November 19, 1975
39.819728, -77.231191; see map N

LOUISIANA

449. Louisiana State Monument

The work of sculptor Donald De Lue (who also created the Mississippi and the Soldiers and Sailors of the Confederacy monuments), the Louisiana State Monument was dedicated in 1971. The dying soldier is from Louisiana's Washington Artillery; the soaring figure is the Spirit of the Confederacy. Louisiana seceded from the Union on January 26, 1861, and contributed around 56,000 soldiers to the Confederate armies. Some 7,000 of them died during the war.

Dedicated in 1971
39.80297, -77.255865; see map U

MAINE

413. 1st Maine Cavalry

According to *Maine at Gettysburg*, "The First Maine was not called into active service during the cavalry battle this afternoon [July 3] until near the close, when it was ordered forward at the termination of the fight."

Dedicated in 1889
39.817926, -77.169324; see map T

80. 2nd Maine Battery (Hall's Battery)

Made of granite from Hallowell, Maine, the 2nd Maine Battery monument indicates the unit's position on July 1. With Capt. James A. Hall of Damariscotta in command and with six 3-inch rifles, the battery arrived shortly after the lead elements of the 1st Corps and "at once opened upon the enemy the first cannonade after the arrival of the Union infantry." The battery also has a marker in Evergreen Cemetery.

Dedicated in 1889
39.837885, -77.251519; see map G

277. 2nd Maine Battery (Hall's Battery)

The battery has a larger monument on Chambersburg Pike, where it fought on July 1. Posted on the left of the artillery on Cemetery Hill, the battery resumed firing in the late afternoon on July 2 with the axle of one cannon breaking from the recoil. The battery moved to the rear to make repairs.

39.817402, -77.231519; see map N

436. 3rd Maine Infantry

Before noon on July 2, the 3rd Maine moved forward toward the Emmitsburg Road to support Berdan's sharpshooters. There it encountered Alabamians of Wilcox's brigade. After a brisk fight in which the 3rd suffered 48 casualties, the Mainers withdrew.

39.808119, -77.257441; see map U

649. 3rd Maine Infantry

Originally commanded by Oliver O. Howard, the 3rd Maine was under Col. Moses B. Lakeman on July 2. After encountering Wilcox's brigade during a morning reconnaissance (there's a marker in Pitzer Woods where the incident occured), the regiment withdrew to the Peach Orchard, where later in the day, it was attacked from two directions amid a "withering fire," and forced to withdraw, along with the rest of the shattered 3rd Corps.

Dedicated in 1889
39.800314, -77.250154; see map AA

536. 3rd Maine Infantry

This marker, made of Maine granite, indicates the 3rd Maine's position on July 3. A marker on Berdan Avenue and a monument near the Peach Orchard commemorate its actions on July 2.

39.812731, -77.235186; see map W

758. 4th Maine Infantry

As fighting raged on Little Round Top, Alabama troops attacked the 4th Maine, which resisted fiercely. "The monument is placed in the gorge of Devil's Den, where the regiment suffered its heaviest loss," notes *Maine at Gettysburg*. "With one of the huge bowlders of that wild place for its foundation, it is a conspicuous memorial of Maine valor."

Dedicated in 1988
39.791858, -77.241498; see map BB

541. 4th Maine Infantry

After its severe fighting at Devil's Den (where its main monument stands) on July 2, the 4th Maine withdrew to a reserve position. On July 3, it moved here to support the 2nd Corps. "The enemy, however, had just been repulsed, and the regiment was not actively engaged," reports *Maine at Gettysburg*.

39.812467, -77.235379 ; see map W

791. 5th Maine Infantry

Mustered in Portland, Maine, the men of the 5th Maine had fought at First Bull Run, but at Gettysburg "by the fortunes of the day they were spared hard fighting and heavy losses."

Dedicated in 1889
39.795372, -77.235158; see map CC

131. 5th Maine Battery (Stevens's Battery)

During the fighting on July 1, the 5th Maine Battery moved its six guns north to this spot. Forced to withdraw, the unit nearly lost a gun when a wheel fell off the carriage, but prompt action by Capt. Greenleaf Stevens saved it. The battery's main monument is on Stevens Knoll, named after the 5th Maine's captain.

39.833813, -77.245022; see map H

312. 5th Maine Battery (Stevens's Battery)

Capt. Greenleaf Thurlow Stevens, for whom Stevens Knoll is named, commanded the 5th Maine Battery here. The battery supported the repulse of Jubal Early's men on the evening of July 2, opening up on the charging Confederates with "blaze, a crash and a roar as if a volcano had been let loose."

Dedicated in 1889
39.819298, -77.224541; see map O

619. 6th Maine Battery (Dow's Battery)

Commanded by Lt. Edwin B. Dow, the 6th Maine reached the battlefield on the morning of July 2. Around 7:00 that evening, it was ordered forward to help stop the advancing Confederates and "hold the position at all hazards." Dow and his men labored under severe fire until the enemy was repulsed. The monument is constructed of Hallowell granite.

Dedicated in 1889
39.80328, -77.234511; see map W

843. 6th Maine Infantry

Arriving on the field on July 2, the 6th Maine was held in reserve and on July 3 went to the left, "part of a force intended to frustrate any attempt of the Confederates to get into the rear of the Union army," recounts *Maine at Gettysburg.*

Dedicated in 1889
39.783432, -77.228409; see map GG

637. 7th Maine Infantry

After the 7th Maine reached this spot on July 3, the regiment advanced toward a house that sheltered enemy skirmishers. "It was in this advance and in a sharp skirmish to the left that the Seventh met its loss at Gettysburg," read a history. "Two men were killed or mortally wounded, and five wounded." The regiment continued skirmishing here for the rest of the day.

Dedicated in 1889
39.807734, -77.210862; see map Y

629. 10th Maine Battalion

Made up from men of the 10th Maine after that regiment mustered out in April 1863, the battalion served as provost guard for the 12th Corps. The monument to the 10th Maine Battalion was crafted of granite from Hallowell, Maine.

Dedicated in 1889
39.811518, -77.220723; see map X

34. 16th Maine Infantry

The 16th Maine reached the field on July 1—about 275 men under Col. Charles W. Tilden—and moved forward to support the beleaguered men of Baxter's brigade. Fighting was intense until the Union forces had to withdraw; the 16th Maine received orders to move forward and hold their position to allow the rest of the division to retreat safely. Tilden was among those captured, but he managed to escape from Richmond's Libby Prison.

Dedicated in 1889
39.841516, -77.242819; see map B

20. 16th Maine Infantry

The 16th Maine's monument is further down Doubleday Road. This marker indicates where the regiment moved after 4:00 pm on July 1 when ordered to hold the position "at any cost" so the rest of the division could withdraw. Most of the soldiers were killed or captured, but not before tearing their flags to pieces and hiding the remnants among themselves to keep them from falling into enemy hands.

39.844527, -77.241995; see map B

706. 17th Maine Infantry

The 17th Maine made a stubborn resistance in the Wheatfield on July 2 by the stone wall here (as shown atop the monument). "The regiment took position just in time to receive the first and furious attack made by the enemy on that part of the line," read a history. The fight became "a desperate struggle at close quarters" until, out of ammunition, the 17th Maine received orders to pull back.

Dedicated in 1888
39.795701, -77.244461; see map BB

577. 17th Maine Infantry

This is the smaller of two monuments to the 17th Maine and indicates the regiment's position on July 3. It is made of Maine granite. The other monument is in the Wheatfield, where the regiment fought on July 2.

39.807992, -77.236081; see map W

553. 19th Maine Infantry

At the height of the battle on July 3, the 19th Maine rushed to their right to support the Union center. "It was a wild charge, with little regard for ranks or files." Its colonel, Francis E. Heath, was wounded. Lt. Col. Henry W. Cunningham of Belfast took over, and the regiment helped repulse the rebels from the Copse of Trees.

Dedicated in 1889
39.811111, -77.236034; see map W

814. 20th Maine Infantry

The 20th Maine held the far left of Strong Vincent's brigade on Little Round Top. "No, I never expected to leave that hill alive," its commander, Col. Joshua Lawrence Chamberlain, later said. Vincent told Chamberlain to hold the position "at all hazards" and the regiment's stubborn defense has become the stuff of legend, thanks in part to its role in Michael Shaara's novel *The Killer Angels* and *Gettysburg*, the movie based on it.

Dedicated in 1886
39.789382, -77.236085; see map CC

834. 20th Maine Infantry

The 20th Maine's best-known monument is on the south side of Little Round Top. Following the fighting there, late on July 2, the regiment moved with the rest of the 3rd Brigade to the top of Big Round Top, where it established a defensive position.

Dedicated in 1889
39.786465, -77.239507; see map FF

817. 20th Maine Infantry, Company B

Capt. Walter G. Morrill had taken Company B of the 20th Maine out as skirmishers. He found himself isolated from the rest of the regiment when the 47th Alabama attacked. Reinforced by some sharpshooters, Company B took a defensive position behind a stone wall.

39.7887, -77.23485; see map CC

669. Maine Sharpshooters (Company D, 2nd United States Sharpshooters)

Under Capt. Jacob McClure of Rockland, on July 2, the Maine sharpshooters moved forward from their position north of Little Round Top toward the Emmitsburg Road, stopping near the Slyder farm. As Hood's advancing Confederates threatened their flank, the sharpshooters kept up "a vigorous fire" as they retired toward Devil's Den, where some of them later fell captive.

Dedicated in 1889
39.790596, -77.249679; see map AA

MARYLAND

368. 1st Maryland (Potomac Home Brigade)

Early on July 3, the 1st Maryland, commanded by Col. William Maulsby, received orders to attack the enemy in front of them. They moved forward under "a severe musketry fire" until, "having already lost in killed and wounded some 80 men," their brigade commander ordered the regiment back.

Dedicated in 1888
39.814818, -77.216927; see map O

405. 1st Maryland Cavalry

The 1st Maryland Cavalry operated in a reserve capacity in a clover field near the Lott house during the great cavalry battle on July 3.

Dedicated in 1888
39.825157, -77.16301; see map S

639. 1st Maryland Light Artillery, Battery A (Rigby's Maryland Baltimore Artillery)

"This battery had six rifled guns, and lay on Power's Hill, with a battery of six Parrott Guns on its left," noted historian John Bachelder. "I have been informed by Major-General Slocum that the battery did terrible execution," reported its commander, James H. Rigby—terrible in terms of its effect on the enemy, not its ability.

Dedicated in 1888
39.80611, -77.219581; see map Y

328. 1st Regiment Eastern Shore Maryland Infantry

Part of Henry H. Lockwood's unattached brigade of the 12th Corps, the 1st Regiment Eastern Shore Maryland Infantry was a Union regiment, though its colonel, James Wallace, owned slaves. Some of its soldiers had left to join the Confederates. The regiment was still green when it reached Gettysburg on the morning of July 3.

Dedicated in 1888
39.819189, -77.21967; see map O

354. 2nd Maryland Infantry, C.S.A.

The monument to the 2nd Maryland Infantry was the first Confederate monument erected on the battlefield, not without controversy. As a Gettysburg Battlefield Memorial Association member wrote on the topic, "The historical delineation of the field is one thing, the erection of monuments in honor of what was done here, is quite another thing." Although the unit fought here as the 1st Maryland Battalion, it was commemorated as the 2nd Maryland (although someone chiseled in an unofficial correction on the monument).

Dedicated in 1886
39.816633, -77.218285; see map O

351. 2nd Maryland Infantry, C.S.A. (1st Maryland Battalion)

This small marker indicates the Confederate 1st Maryland Battalion's furthest advance. The unit's main monument, labeled the 2nd Maryland Infantry, C.S.A., is nearby. Marylander fought Marylander here on Culp's Hill.

39.816519, -77.21954; see map O

361. 3rd Maryland Infantry

Col. Joseph M. Sudsburg of the 3rd Maryland Infantry reported, "[M]y regiment was engaged, July 2, at Gettysburg on the extreme right of the line, but in the evening we were ordered to the left, where we remained about one hour, when we returned to occupy our former position, but found the enemy had taken possession."

Dedicated in 1888
39.815618, –77.217655; see map O

401. Purnell Legion, Maryland Cavalry

There were three companies in the Purnell Legion battalion of cavalry, but instead of serving together as a single unit they served separately on special duty. Company A was with the Army of the Potomac during the Gettysburg campaign.

Dedicated in 1888
39.826485, –77.164623; see map S

289. Maryland State Monument

Maryland was a slave state and a border state with divided loyalties. Soldiers from Maryland joined both sides in the conflict. At Gettysburg some 3,000 Marylanders fought in the battle—for both the Union and the Confederacy. As a Union soldier recalled after one such encounter on Culp's Hill, "We sorrowfully gathered up many of our old friends & acquaintances & had them carefully & tenderly cared for."

Dedicated in 1994–1995
39.816278, –77.232674; see map N

MASSACHUSETTS

787. 1st Massachusetts Cavalry

Appropriately, the 1st Massachusetts Cavalry monument stands near the statue of John Sedgwick; it served with that general's 6th Corps headquarters during the battle.

Dedicated in 1885
39.796018, -77.234219; see map CC

478. 1st Massachusetts Infantry

The 1st Massachusetts was with Gen. Humphreys's division in the 3rd Corps' stretched-thin line when the enemy attacked on July 2. "For a short time the fighting was furious, but the enemy's three lines of battle proving too much for our one, we were obliged to give way before much superior odds," reported Lt. Col. Clark B. Baldwin, the regiment's commander.

Dedicated in 1886
39.808744, -77.243696; see map V

479. 1st Massachusetts Infantry

This marker indicates the position of the 1st Massachusetts's skirmishers when they advanced beyond the Emmitsburg Road on July 2. The regiment's main monument is on the Emmitsburg Road, about 200 yards to the east.

39.810927, -77.245032; see map V

275. 1ˢᵗ Massachusetts Light Artillery, Battery A (McCartney's Battery)

Held in reserve for most of the battle, Battery A of the 1ˢᵗ Massachusetts Light Artillery, under the command of Capt. William H. McCartney, received orders to go into action on July 3, "but by some error it first went to the left, and only returned to the point where it was needed in time to fire a few shots at the retreating Confederates."

Dedicated in 1885
39.817697, -77.231581; see map N

220. 1ˢᵗ Massachusetts Sharpshooters (Andrew Sharpshooters)

"In God we put our trust / but kept our powder dry," says this monument to the 1ˢᵗ Massachusetts Sharpshooters. They were also known as the Andrew Sharpshooters, after the wartime governor of the commonwealth of Massachusetts, John A. Andrew.

39.813656, -77.235448; see map M

279. 1ˢᵗ Massachusetts Sharpshooters (Andrew Sharpshooters)

The 1ˢᵗ Massachusetts Sharpshooters have their main monument on Hancock Avenue. After the war, L. E. Bicknell recalled entering Ziegler's Grove with about 20 of his men on July 3 and fending off enemy sharpshooters until the Confederate cannonade began.

39.817069, -77.234114; see map N

694. 2nd Company, Massachusetts Sharpshooters (Andrew Sharpshooters)

The monument to the 2nd Company of the Massachusetts Sharpshooters has unfortunately been a magnet for vandals. On one occasion, it was sprayed with blue paint; on another, someone knocked the head off. On the latter occasion, a park ranger on night patrol "was surprised to see the headless human likeness illuminated by the patrol car headlights," according to a newspaper account.

Dedicated in 1885
39.796929, -77.246335; see map BB

375. 2nd Massachusetts Infantry

Ordered to take the 2nd Massachusetts on an ill-advised charge here, Lt. Col. Charles Mudge said, "It is murder but it is an order." Mudge died in the attack. Remembered Brig. Gen. Alpheus S. Williams, "There are few if any regts. in the service that could have stood the almost instantaneous loss of half its force and maintained, as the 2d Mass. did, almost perfectly the order and regularity of a battalion drill."

Dedicated in 1879
39.813432, -77.216149; see map O

770. 3rd Massachusetts Battery (Walcott's Battery)

Known as Walcott's Battery after its commander, Lt. Aaron F. Walcott (and also as Battery C, Massachusetts Light Artillery), the 3rd Massachusetts Battery had six 12-pound guns and served with the artillery reserve of the 5th Corps.

Dedicated in 1885
39.796698, -77.2381; see map CC

514. 5th Massachusetts Battery (Phillips's Battery)

An account of the 5th Massachusetts Battery reported, "On the 13th of June this command began its march toward Gettysburg, where it arrived on July 2. On this and the succeeding day, the battery was in action, losing seven killed and thirteen wounded. Fifty-nine horses were disabled, and seven hundred rounds were fired."

Dedicated in 1885
39.800582, -77.246902; see map V

788. 7th Massachusetts Infantry

The 7th Massachusetts Infantry served near this spot on July 2, moving "from point to point with its brigade, often under fire, but fortunately escaping without loss," read a history.

Dedicated in 1885
39.795984, -77.23412; see map CC

515. 9th Massachusetts Battery (Bigelow's Battery)

The 9th Massachusetts Battery, under Capt. John Bigelow, wreaked havoc on McLaws's advancing Confederates on July 2 until told to withdraw. Bigelow used the recoil of his cannons to gradually move back while "damaging as much as possible the approaching line of battle with spherical case shot" until he reached the Trostle barn. The battery has another monument there.

Dedicated in 1885
39.800116, -77.245613; see map V

519. 9th Massachusetts Battery (Bigelow's Battery)

Under the command of Capt. John Bigelow, the 9th Massachusetts Battery was pushed back to this spot from the Peach Orchard on July 2. As the battery prepared to move back again it received orders to hold the position "at all hazards." During the ensuing fighting, the battery lost four of its six guns but performed a vital delaying action. The dead horses it left behind are visible in photographs taken after the battle.

Dedicated in 1885
39.801671, -77.24253; see map V

202. 9th Massachusetts Battery (Bigelow's Battery)

The 9th Massachusetts Battery has three monuments on the battlefield. The battery had started the battle with six guns but, after a heroic rearguard action on July 2, had only two remaining for the fighting here on July 3.

Dedicated in 1885
39.815857, -77.234905; see map M

764. 9th Massachusetts Infantry

The 9th Massachusetts was sent as pickets to the Union left "and in the duties of that position and skirmishing it was engaged during the battle, suffering a loss of but one killed and three wounded."

Dedicated in 1885
39.788476, -77.23779; see map BB

783. 10ᵗʰ Massachusetts Infantry

Vandals damaged the monument to the 10ᵗʰ Massachusetts, tearing the bronze muskets from its top; money is being raised for its repair. "The brigade being in reserve, though doing much marching back and forth along the line and frequently exposed to fire, the Tenth lost but one man killed and three wounded during the battle," notes *Massachusetts in the War, 1861-1865.*

39.796389, -77.234265; see map CC

482. 11ᵗʰ Massachusetts Infantry

In the fighting on July 2, the 11ᵗʰ Massachusetts, commanded by Lt. Col. Porter D. Tripp, "suffered terribly, losing more than half the number taken into action." In 2006, its monument suffered when vandals tore off the arm and sword from the top.

Dedicated in 1885
39.808079, -77.243968; see map V

22. 12ᵗʰ Massachusetts Infantry (The Webster Regiment)

The 12ᵗʰ Massachusetts' monument bears a portrait of Daniel Webster but was named after his son, Daniel Fletcher Webster, its first commander. Webster the son died at Antietam. On July 1, the regiment ran out of ammunition and stood with fixed bayonets, "exposed to the enemy's fire of artillery and infantry, without the power to return a shot," until forced to withdraw. There are smaller regimental markers on Hancock Avenue and in Ziegler's Grove.

39.843652, -77.242139; see map B

602. 12th Massachusetts Infantry (Webster Regiment)

This modest stone marks the 12th Massachusetts's location on July 2, when it served as a reserve for the 2nd and 11th Corps. Two other monuments—on Doubleday Avenue and in Ziegler's Grove—indicate where the regiment fought on July 1 and 3.

39.806738, -77.235103; see map W

281. 12th Massachusetts Infantry (Webster Regiment)

The regiment's main monument is on Doubleday Avenue. This one indicates its location late on July 3, when it was ordered forward to support the 2nd Corps "and arrived just in time to witness the repulse of the enemy."

39.817083, -77.233819; see map N

28. 13th Massachusetts Infantry

During the fighting here on July 1, the 13th Massachusetts fired into advancing North Carolina troops. "Give it to 'em for Fredericksburg!" yelled the New England soldiers. Soon, though, the Union 11th Corps on the right collapsed, forcing a retreat of the entire federal line.

Dedicated in 1885
39.842727, -77.241354; see map B

556. 15th Massachusetts Infantry

On July 2, John Gibbon sent the 15th Massachusetts forward to support Daniel Sickles's exposed 3rd Corps; their colonel, George H. Ward, was mortally wounded during the fighting. On July 3, the regiment moved to its right to aid in the Confederate repulse, where "it fought nobly, though at heavy loss of officers and men."

Dedicated in 1885
39.810799, -77.236093; see map W

488. 16th Massachusetts Infantry

The 16th Massachusetts took a beating on July 2. "In the terrible conflict of that afternoon the regiment fought nobly, losing fully one-third of its members present, but being forced back with the rest of its division," according to *Massachusetts in the War, 1861–1865*.

Dedicated in 1886
39.807044, -77.245382; see map V

690. 18th Massachusetts Infantry

A history of Massachusetts regiments modestly described the role of the 18th Massachusetts: "The part taken in the battle of Gettysburg by the Eighteenth was like that at Chancellorsville, not important, and by a coincidence the loss on the two fields was the same—one killed and 13 wounded."

Dedicated in 1885
39.797331, -77.245924; see map BB

551. 19th Massachusetts Infantry

At the climax of the Confederate attack on July 3, Gen. Hancock rode up to Col. Arthur Devereux, pointed to the Confederates approaching the Copse of Trees, and told him "to get in God Damn quick." The 19th Massachusetts and 42nd New York both charged into the thick of the fighting and participated in the final repulse of the rebels.

Dedicated in 1885
39.811478, -77.235515; see map W

550. 20th Massachusetts Infantry (Harvard Regiment)

One of the more unusual monuments, this piece of Massachusetts "puddingstone" is supposed to represent the local rocks the soldiers climbed on as children. Known as the Harvard Regiment, the 20th Massachusetts was commanded by Col. Paul Revere, grandson of the famed horseman, until he fell to a mortal wound on July 2. His replacement, Col. George Macy, was badly wounded in the fierce, close fighting here on July 3.

Dedicated in 1885
39.81147, -77.236162; see map W

688. 22nd Massachusetts Infantry (Henry Wilson's Regiment)

Part of a brigade raised by senator Henry Wilson, the 22nd Massachusetts "fought with an energy and a coolness worthy of all praise." When forced to retreat, it "did so in good order, bringing off all its wounded and even their weapons."

Dedicated in 1885
39.797051, -77.246465; see map BB

691. 28th Massachusetts Infantry

The 28th Massachusetts was one of the regiments of the Irish Brigade. As part of Caldwell's division of the 2nd Corps, it advanced to support the retreating 3rd Corps. "A fine attack was delivered, and the enemy driven back, but the flanks of the assaulting column were not covered and were soon almost enveloped by the Confederates," says to a history of Massachusetts in the war. "Faugh a Ballagh" ("Clear the Way") is an Irish battle cry.

Dedicated in 1885
39.797352, -77.245731; see map BB

698. 32nd Massachusetts Field Hospital

Zabdiel Boylston Adams of Framingham, Massachusetts, served as the regimental surgeon for the 32nd Massachusetts. On July 2, he established his field hospital behind the shelter provided by the boulders here. He had plenty of work: On July 2, the regiment suffered 79 killed and wounded.

39.797183, -77.244985; see map BB

695. 32nd Massachusetts Infantry

One of the more unusual monuments on the battlefield, that of the 32nd Massachusetts depicts a soldier's tent. Sent as part of the 5th Corps to support the collapsing 3rd, the 32nd and its brigade were forced to make a fighting retreat, "losing heavily till they reached the woods in the rear of the field, where Lieutenant Colonel Stephenson was badly wounded through the face."

Dedicated in 1885
39.796952, -77.245989; see map BB

259. 33rd Massachusetts Infantry

In the growing dusk of July 2, the 33rd Massachusetts waited behind a stone wall for Avery's North Carolinians. "My regiment opened a severe musketry fire on them, which caused gaps in their line and made it stagger back a little," reported Col. Adin Underwood. Finally, the rebels retreated, "leaving great heaps of dead and wounded just in front of us."

Dedicated in 1885
39.819861, -77.226179; see map N

780. 37th Massachusetts Infantry

After taking part in the 6th Corps' long march to the battlefield, the 37th Massachusetts went into battle late in the afternoon on July 2, but suffered relatively light casualties, with 2 killed, 26 wounded, and 19 more missing.

Dedicated in 1885
39.797295, -77.234511; see map CC

MICHIGAN

685. 1st Michigan Infantry

On July 2, Col. Ira C. Abbott had the men of the 1st Michigan lie on the ground as the enemy approached and then ordered them to stand and fire at the rebels, "which made a dreadful confusion in their ranks and caused them to fall." Abbott said his line remained "firm as a rock" even though his men "fell like sheep before the slaughter" from return fire. Abbott himself was wounded.

Dedicated in 1888
39.797301, -77.246451; see map BB

650. 3rd Michigan Infantry

On July 2, the 3rd Michigan moved forward toward the Emmitsburg Road, where it repulsed initial Confederate attacks. The regiment fought "with a desperation never before witnessed, and at times at a range of not over 50 yards," reported Lt. Col. Edwin S. Pierce, who assumed command when his brother, Col. Byron Root Pierce, was wounded.

Dedicated in 1888
39.800178, -77.249255; see map AA

703. 4th Michigan Infantry

During the fighting for the Wheatfield, Col. Harrison H. Jeffords of the 4th Michigan and two other soldiers attempted to rescue the regimental colors. "The Colonel secured the colors or at least had his hand on the staff," recalled color-bearer Henry S. Seage, "and in the act of fighting their way out, Col. Jeffords was killed, by bayonet thrust through the body." The other two soldiers, one of them Seage's brother, were wounded.

Dedicated in 1889
39.796202, -77.243972; see map BB

699. 5th Michigan Infantry

Around 4:00 pm on July 2, Lt. Col. John Pulford received orders to advance to his brigade's front. There, he said, "I was met by the enemy who attacked my line of skirmishers in force compelling them to fall back on the battalion reserve." The rebels he met were from Kershaw's brigade.

Dedicated in 1888
39.79706, -77.245082; see map BB

545. 7th Michigan Infantry

The 7th Michigan was one of the few Gettysburg regiments equipped with the .54 caliber Burnside carbine, a gun patented by Ambrose Burnside, who went on to command the Army of the Potomac (disastrously) at Fredericksburg. From their position here on July 3, the men were able to use their Burnsides to fire into the flank of the approaching Confederates, although at least part of the regiment broke for the rear.

Dedicated in 1888
39.811843, -77.23631; see map W

578. 9th Michigan Battery
(Daniels's Battery)

The battery was positioned here on July 3 and fired at the enemy for five hours starting at 12:30 pm. "I succeeded in silencing one of the enemy's batteries at 2 pm," reported Captain Jabez J. Daniels. The guns silenced another enemy battery 700 yards away before enemy infantry attempted an attack, which was repulsed.

39.807893, -77.235943; see map W

806. 16th Michigan Infantry

One officer of the 16th Michigan remembered seeing the regiment's commander, Lt. Col. Norval E. Welch, standing with the regimental colors on a large rock "till it was not possible to remain longer in that place." The men returned Confederate fire "with vigor and precision" but some retreated under orders to retire. Attempting to rally them, brigade commander Strong Vincent fell mortally wounded.

Dedicated in 1889
39.79126, -77.237688; see map CC

94. 24th Michigan Infantry

The Iron Brigade's 24th Michigan Infantry suffered the highest losses of any Union regiment at Gettysburg. The regiment outflanked Archer's brigade from the south and then engaged in a fierce fight with the 26th North Carolina in McPherson's Woods. It was "the bloodiest and most stubbornly contested point in all the fighting of that day," said Capt. Albert Edwards, who took command when Col. Henry Morrow was wounded.

Dedicated in 1888
39.834859, -77.25459; see map G

313. 24th Michigan

This marker indicates the position of the 24th Michigan, part of the Iron Brigade, on July 2 and 3. The regiment had been badly hurt during the fighting on July 1, suffering the highest losses of any Union regiment at the battle.

39.819517, -77.224058; see map O

400. Michigan Cavalry Brigade (1st, 5th, 6th, & 7th Michigan Cavalry)

George Armstrong Custer was with Brig. Gen. David McMurtrie Gregg's cavalry division even though he served under Judson Kilpatrick. On July 3, he was at the head of the 7th Michigan. With a cry of "Come on, you Wolverines," Custer led the charge against Jeb Stuart's rebel horsemen and helped blunt the Confederate attempt to get behind the Union lines.

Dedicated in 1889
39.826222, -77.16536; see map S

805. Michigan Sharpshooters

The Michigan Sharpshooters consisted of companies C, I, and K of the 1st United States Sharpshooters and company B of the 2nd United States Sharpshooters.

Dedicated in 1889
39.791814, -77.237733; see map CC

MINNESOTA

603. 1st Minnesota Infantry

The 1st Minnesota has three monuments on the battlefield. This one commemorates a courageous charge at a desperate moment on July 2. Gen. Winfield Scott Hancock noted the enemy moving toward a gap in his line. "Advance, Colonel, and take those colors," he ordered Col. William Colville of the 1st Minnesota. Colville and his regiment delayed the Confederate advance long enough for other Union soldiers to arrive. The regiment suffered 68 percent causalities, including Colville.

Dedicated in 1893
39.806716, -77.235116; see map W

558. 1st Minnesota Infantry

This is the second of three monuments to the regiment. As the survivors of Pickett's Charge neared the Union lines, the regiment received orders to charge their flank. Cpl. Henry O'Brien led the 1st Minnesota with the regimental flag and later received the Medal of Honor. "We just rushed in like wild beasts," recalled one lieutenant. "Men swore and cursed and struggled and fought."

Dedicated in 1898
39.810575, -77.236001; see map W

265. 1st Minnesota Infantry

Placed here in 1867, this monument to the 1st Minnesota can also lay claim to being the battlefield's first because it predated the completion of the Soldiers National Monument by two years. The regiment has two other monuments on the battlefield.

39.819661, -77.231795; see map N

MISSISSIPPI

186. 11th Mississippi Infantry

The monument to the 11th Mississippi, sculpted by William Beckwith, depicts William O'Brien, the color sergeant for Company C. Advancing on the left flank of the Confederate attack on July 3, the regiment suffered terribly, with 340 causalities among its 393 men. A marker off Hancock Avenue near the Brian barn indicates the farthest point the regiment's survivors reached that day.

Dedicated in 2000
39.818789, -77.247693; see map L

206. 11th Mississippi Infantry

Which Confederates advanced the farthest on July 3? Virginians say Armistead and his men did. North Carolinians claim it was the Tarheels of the 26th North Carolina, farther south down Cemetery Ridge. Mississippians say members of the 11th Mississippi claimed the honor. This monument, placed here in 1998, indicates the farthest point of their advance.

Dedicated in 1998
39.815321, -77.235565; see map M

453. Mississippi State Monument

Another work from sculptor Donald De Lue, (who also created the Louisiana monument), the Mississippi State Monument stands on the site where the state's Gen. William Barksdale and his brigade moved out to attack the Union lines on July 2. Barksdale was mortally wounded in the fighting. Mississippi became the second state to leave the Union when it seceded on January 9, 1861; it contributed up to 80,000 soldiers to the Confederacy.

Dedicated in 1973
39.802404, -77.255885; see map U

NEW HAMPSHIRE

274. 1st New Hampshire Battery Light Artillery (Edgell's Battery)

On July 2, Battery A, 1st New Hampshire Artillery, remained in reserve until Battery C, 1st West Virginia Artillery, ran out of ammunition, and Capt. James Huntington ordered the New Hampshire guns forward to take its place. Capt. Frederick M. Edgell was in command. "The casualties in my battery were 3 men wounded (only 1 seriously)," reported Edgell. "I also lost 3 horses killed, and a wheel and axle broken."

Dedicated in 1912
39.817979, -77.232208; see map N

THE ARMIES AT GETTYSBURG

A total of approximately 166,000 soldiers fought at Gettysburg. The Army of the Potomac brought around 94,000 men to the field, outnumbering the 72,000 soldiers of the Army of Northern Virginia. Pennsylvania provided the most soldiers—24,000—out of all of the 18 Union states represented. Virginians numbered almost 21,000, the greatest number from any of the 12 Confederate states that participated at Gettysburg. Most of the men who fought here were from volunteer regiments raised by the states, but a little more than 7,000 regular army soldiers served with the Army of the Potomac.

471. 2nd New Hampshire Infantry

Col. Edward L. Bailey commanded the 2nd New Hampshire. On July 2, as the rebels advanced, enemy batteries "showered upon us a perfect hail of metal," Bailey remembered. The regiments on either side of the battery, the 68th Pennsylvania and the 3rd Maine, retreated. "I was forced to retire," said Bailey. "My own line was afterwards plainly marked by the dead who fell in this position."

Dedicated in 1886
39.800571, -77.250366; see map U

748. 5th New Hampshire Infantry

At 4:30 pm on July 2, Lt. Col. Charles Hapgood of the 5th New Hampshire ordered the regiment to advance at double-quick. It did so, "and at once engaged the enemy in the woods to the left of the wheat-field." During the war, the regiment suffered the most casualties of any federal regiment, losing 295 killed and 756 wounded. Its original colonel, Edward Cross, died at the head of the brigade on July 2.

39.795131, -77.241954; see map BB

490. 12th New Hampshire Infantry

According to its commander, Capt. John F. Langley, the 12th New Hampshire "conducted itself very bravely, promptly obeying orders, and in every movement keeping a good line." As the regiment withdrew, Sgt. William Howe was killed as he defiantly waved the state and national colors at the advancing enemy. Langley was wounded in the fighting.

Dedicated in 1888
39.806505, -77.246043; see map V

576. New Hampshire Sharpshooters

This monument commemorates the New Hampshire companies of the 1st and 2nd U.S. Sharpshooters, also known as Berdan's Sharpshooters. Clad in distinctive green uniforms and equipped with breech-loading Sharps carbines, the sharpshooters aimed to pick off enemy soldiers from a distance—like snipers. The monument indicates where these companies were on July 3.

Dedicated in 1886
39.80808, -77.236197; see map W

NEW JERSEY

395. 1st New Jersey Cavalry

On July 3, finding Jeb Stuart's cavalry occupying the Rummel farm, the 1st New Jersey dismounted and prepared to fight. The Confederates pushed out skirmishers. "The 1st New Jersey soon adjusted their line to correspond with that of their antagonists, and firing began," remembered a U.S. cavalryman.

Dedicated in 1888
39.828629, -77.169917; see map R

582. 1st New Jersey Light Artillery, Battery A (Hexamer's Battery)

This artillery battery galloped into action from its reserve position around 3:00 on the afternoon of July 3 to fire 120 rounds at the advancing Confederates of Pickett's Charge. "At one time during the engagement, the rebels, pressing impetuously forward, were within ten yards" of the battery's guns, read a history, "but not a man flinched for a moment."

Dedicated in 1888
39.807384, -77.235415; see map W

505. 1st New Jersey Light Artillery, Battery B (Clark's Battery)

Col. Freeman McGilvery reported that Battery B of the New Jersey Light Artillery, under the command of Capt. Adoniram Clark, "was receiving the most of the fire of two or more rebel batteries" on July 2. The rebel advance exposed the batteries here to "warm infantry fronts from both flanks and front," so Clark "deemed it best to retire."

39.801363, -77.247198; see map V

626. 1st New Jersey Brigade

Made up of the 1st, 2nd, 3rd, 4th, and 15th New Jersey regiments, the 1st New Jersey Brigade was under the command of Brig. Gen. Alfred Torbert, who has a bronze bas-relief on the monument. Torbert received both Union and Confederate commissions, although he remained loyal to the Union. He later commanded cavalry under Phil Sheridan. The other bronze portrait is of the brigade's former commander, Philip Kearny, who was killed at Chantilly, Virginia, on September 1, 1862.

39.800662, -77.23348; see map W

641. 4th New Jersey Infantry

The 4th New Jersey served as a guard for the ammunition trains and as provost guard on July 2 and 3. "The part taken by the regiment was insignificant," reported Maj. Charles Ewing, until it had to deploy across the road with fixed bayonets to stop soldiers fleeing from the oncoming rebels of Pickett's Charge on July 3.

Dedicated in 1888
39.804715, -77.218052; see map Y

484. 5th New Jersey Infantry

The 5th New Jersey was supporting Battery K of the 4th U.S. Artillery on July 2 when the enemy opened up with "a tempest of battle-hail." Under the onslaught, the regiment was compelled to withdraw, and its colonel, William J. Sewell, was badly wounded.

Dedicated in 1888
39.80744, -77.245178; see map V

747. 6th New Jersey Infantry

The 6th New Jersey, under the command of Lt. Col. Stephen Gilkyson, was detached from its brigade and sent into Devil's Den. "Here we secured a fine position, and opened fire with great effect, driving the enemy from our immediate front, remaining in this position for about two hours, being during this time actively engaged," reported Gilkyson.

Dedicated in 1888
39.793343, -77.240834; see map BB

507. 7th New Jersey Infantry

The 7th New Jersey was here when the rebels unleashed an artillery barrage on the afternoon of July 2. "Many of the shells burst directly over the regiment and several men were killed as they lay in the ranks." Cpl. Eugene Pollard was struck in the neck and left for dead, but he recovered and afterwards kept the shell fragment the surgeons removed in his pocket.

Dedicated in 1888
39.801462, -77.246771; see map V

709. 8th New Jersey Infantry

The 8th New Jersey fought in the Wheatfield on July 2. Its brigade commander, George C. Burling, recalled how the regiment, along with the 6th New Jersey and the 115th Pennsylvania, "charged across a wheat field, clearing it of the enemy. . . . Eventually we were all driven back from this advanced position."

Dedicated in 1888
39.795999, -77.245548; see map BB

492. 11th New Jersey Infantry

On July 2, William Barksdale's Mississippians advanced, pushing in the skirmishers of the 11th New Jersey. "Up to this time the Eleventh had not fired a single shot, but as the enemy pressed forward upon our lines, Colonel [Robert] McAllister gave the order, and, at the same moment, fell severely wounded by a Minie ball in his left leg, and a piece of shell in the right foot." The regiment had to retire.

Dedicated in 1888
39.805935, -77.246619; see map V

208. 12th New Jersey Infantry

The bronze bas-relief depicts the regiment's action of July 3 to capture the Bliss barn, a structure being used by Confederate sharpshooters. Following orders from Gen. Hancock to take the barn, the regiment's commander, Maj. John T. Hill, sent four companies forward to accomplish that task. (The regiment also has a marker there.) On July 3, the regiment helped repulse the Confederate assault from behind the stone wall here.

Dedicated in 1886
39.815142, -77.235482; see map M

196. 12th New Jersey Infantry

On July 3, the 12th New Jersey moved forward to this spot to drive rebels from the Bliss farm buildings. A bronze bas-relief on the regiment's main monument on Hancock Avenue depicts the fighting here.

39.816582, -77.241928; see map M

381. 13th New Jersey Infantry

From this position on July 3, the 13th New Jersey, under the command of Col. Ezra Carman (who would later publish an important work on Antietam), suffered from the irritating fire of sharpshooters in the Z. Taney house across Rock Creek. Artillery cleared out the rebels, but they eventually returned.

Dedicated in 1887
39.813121, -77.214634; see map P

NEW YORK

559. 1st New York Light Artillery, Battery B (Pettit's Battery)

Organized under Capt. Rufus T. Pettit in Elmira, New York, at Gettysburg the battery was commanded by Lt. Albert S. Sheldon and then by Capt. James McKay Rorty. The battery suffered terribly under the Confederate cannonade on July 3, which killed Rorty and badly wounded Sheldon. Members of the 19th Massachusetts Infantry pitched in to help work the guns.

39.810631, -77.235907; see map W

789. 1st New York Light Artillery, Battery C

Battery C of the New York Light Artillery was positioned here under the command of Capt. Almont Barnes on July 2. "With remarkable good fortune his battery escaped loss in men and horses, although some of the harness, etc., was cut with bullets and had to be replaced at once."

Dedicated in 1893
39.795944, -77.234799; see map CC

719. 1st New York Light Artillery, Battery D (Winslow's Battery)

Under the command of Capt. George Winslow, Battery D of the 1st New York Light Artillery held off the Confederates in the Wheatfield on July 2 until its infantry support retired. "I withdrew my guns, one at a time, from the left," Winslow reported, "keeping up the fire of the remaining pieces until the last withdrew."

Dedicated in 1888
39.797376, -77.242843; see map BB

258. 1st New York Light Artillery, Battery E & L (Reynolds's Battery)

Although Battery L of the 1st New York Light Artillery was known as Reynolds's battery, Capt. Gilbert Reynolds fell wounded on July 1 and Lt. George Breck had command here on July 2. Breck noted that the cemetery "now is trodden down, laid a waste, desecrated." Battery E was attached to Battery L.

Dedicated in 1891
39.820633, -77.228341; see map N

463. 1st New York Light Artillery, Battery G (Ames's Battery)

Battery G of the 1st New York Light Artillery, under the command of Capt. Nelson Ames, had its guns posted in the Peach Orchard, two guns aiming west and the remainder south, as it dueled with a pair of rebel batteries. Ames reported that "for a short time I had as sharp an artillery fight as I ever witnessed."

Dedicated in 1893
39.801321, -77.25012; see map U

620. 1st New York Light Artillery, Battery G (Ames's Battery)

The battery's main monument is in the Peach Orchard, where it fought on July 2. This smaller marker indicates is position on July 3, when, as a regimental history noted, "we were in position with the Second Corps on the front line of battle, and took part in the terrible artillery duel, also in repelling Pickett's charge, and thus ending one of the most fearful battles of the war."

39.802842, -77.234467; see map W

230. 1st New York Light Artillery, Battery I (Weidrich's Battery)

"I saw that my position could not be held, and had ordered my battery to limber up and fall back to the Baltimore pike, when the Seventy-third and the Twenty-seventh Regiments Pennsylvania Volunteers came to my rescue and repulsed the rebels," said Capt. Michael Wiedrich of the fighting here to save his battery. The struggle took place in the darkness on July 2.

Dedicated in 1889
39.821978, -77.229095; see map N

221. 1ˢᵗ New York Light Artillery, Battery K (Fitzhugh's Battery)

Positioned here on July 3, the guns of the battery "went into position, with the horses on the gallop," and they "did good service in assisting to repel Pickett's charge," at the cost of seven wounded men.

Dedicated in 1888
39.813642, –77.235212; see map M

113. 1ˢᵗ New York Light Artillery, Battery L (Reynolds's Battery)

The circle atop the monument represents the badge of the 1ˢᵗ Corps. The "Reynolds" was Capt. Gilbert Reynolds, who commanded the battery until he was wounded and Lt. George Breck took over. During the withdrawal from Seminary Ridge, the battery had to abandon a disabled gun, which was captured.

Dedicated in 1889
39.834644, –77.250205; see map G

630. 1ˢᵗ New York Light Artillery, Battery M (Winegar's Battery)

According to a unit history, Battery M of the New York Light Artillery on Power's Hill was more to the left and forward of the monument's position. From there the gunners participated in the repulse of the Confederate attack on Culp's Hill by firing at enemy artillery on Benner's Hill. They later moved forward to shell sharpshooters in the Z. Taney house on Rock Creek.

Dedicated in 1889
39.806852, –77.220221; see map X

542. 1ˢᵗ New York Independent Battery (Cowan's Battery)

Under the command of Capt. Andrew Cowan, the battery had six 3-inch ordnance rifles. Ordered to relocate from a position to the left, the battery redeployed here under the eye of Brig. Gen. Alexander Webb.

Dedicated in 1887
39.812395, -77.23551 ; see map W

587. 2ⁿᵈ New York Cavalry

The 2ⁿᵈ New York Cavalry did not actually fight here, having been sent to Manchester, Maryland. After the battle, it joined Judson Kilpatrick's division to attack Lee's retreating columns.

Dedicated in 1892
39.808732, -77.23449; see map W

288. 3ʳᵈ New York Independent Battery (Harn's Battery)

Originally mustered in as a howitzer company of the 2ⁿᵈ Militia Infantry, the unit was later reorganized as a battery of light artillery. Under the command of Capt. William Harn and with six 10-pound Parrotts, the battery participated in the 6ᵗʰ Corps' 36-mile overnight march to reach the battlefield on July 2.

39.81675, -77.232264; see map N

588. 4ᵗʰ New York Cavalry

The 4ᵗʰ New York Cavalry went into Maryland after fighting with Jeb Stuart in Hanover. "Following the retreating enemy to Middleburg and Upperville the regiment made several charges, in one of which—at the latter place—General Kilpatrick was rescued from the enemy's hands by a squadron led by Captain Mann, after being abandoned by another regiment with which General Kilpatrick had charged," read a regimental history.

Dedicated in 1889
39.808352, -77.234615; see map W

756. 4ᵗʰ New York Independent Battery (Smith's Battery)

James E. Smith's 4ᵗʰ New York Independent Battery had four 10-pound Parrott guns. During the fierce combat with Texas soldiers here, Smith lost twelve men, eleven horses, and three of his cannon. Vandals once tore the statue off the monument but it has been replaced, at a cost of at least 30,000 dollars.

Dedicated in 1888
39.791987, -77.242502; see map BB

831. 5ᵗʰ New York Cavalry (1ˢᵗ Ira Harris Guard)

The 5ᵗʰ New York Cavalry supported an artillery battery as Elon Farnsworth made his fatal charge on July 3. "During this charge a shell passed through the body of Daniel Hurley, Company C, killed a horse, and afterward exploded, wounding John Buckley of the same company, and several others," said a regimental history.

Dedicated in 1888
39.783087, -77.246565; see map EE

250. 5th New York Independent Battery (Taft's Battery, 1st Excelsior Light Artillery)

Capt. Elijah Taft commanded the 5th New York Independent Battery, which reached the battlefield on July 2 and used four guns to duel with Confederate batteries to the north and two guns to fire to the west. One of the battery's guns burst at the muzzle during the fighting.

Dedicated in 1888–1889
39.820857, -77.229929; see map N

3. 6th New York Cavalry (Ira Harris Guard)

This elaborate monument paid the price for its size when lightning struck and damaged it in 2007 (it has since been restored). The bronze relief portrait on the reverse portrays Col. Thomas Devin, the regiment's first commander. The scene on the front is titled "General Fitzhugh's Charge," an incident that probably took place not at Gettysburg but at the 1865 Battle of Five Forks. The sculptor was James E. Kelley.

Dedicated in 1889
39.844653, -77.24702; see map B

292. 6th Independent Battery, New York Artillery

Although the 6th Independent Battery of the New York Artillery saw service throughout the war, it was not actively engaged during the Battle of Gettysburg. It was posted here north of Gen. Meade's headquarters.

Dedicated in 1891
39.815604, -77.232091; see map N

117. 8th New York Cavalry

The 8th New York contributed to the spirited defense thrown up by John Buford's cavalry on July 1. After being forced to withdraw to Seminary Ridge, the cavalry performed an equally important delaying action while the 1st Corps retreated to Cemetery Hill.

Dedicated in 1889
39.833569, -77.250552; see map G

5. 9th New York Cavalry

"Discovering the Enemy," the bas-relief sculpture on the front of the 9th New York Calvary's monument, is by Caspar Buberl. The reverse side has a portrait of the regiment's commander, Col. William Sackett, who died at the Battle of Trevilian Station in 1865. Cpl. Alpheus Hodges of the regiment claimed to have fired the battle's first shot (a claim disputed by the 8th Illinois Cavalry).

Dedicated in 1888
39.845603, -77.246389; see map B

382. 10th New York Cavalry

Part of J. Irvin Gregg's brigade of cavalry, the 10th New York served in a reserve capacity during the cavalry battle on July 3 "but lost several men, wounded, nevertheless."

Dedicated in 1888
39.822502, -77.190339; see map Q

513. 10th New York Independent Battery (Lewis's Battery)

"At Gettysburg the Tenth New York was attached to Phillips' Fifth Massachusetts Battery and with that command fought in the battles of the second and third day," read a history from a New York monuments commission.

Dedicated in 1893
39.800634, -77.24714; see map V

295. 10th New York Infantry

The 10th New York Infantry was here on July 3 when it served as provost guard to Alexander Hays's division of the Union 2nd Corps. Maj. George F. Hooper, the regiment's commander, reported taking change of some 1,800 rebel prisoners.

Dedicated in 1889
39.81426, -77.234441; see map N

219. 11th Independent (Havelock) Battery, New York Light Artillery

Formed from two batteries that were consolidated in 1862, the 11th had served with a number of units before it was attached to Battery K of the 1st New York Light Artillery prior to Gettysburg. It had two 3-inch ordnance rifles.

Dedicated in 1893
39.813718, -77.235258; see map M

51. 13th New York Independent Battery (Wheeler's Battery)

Commanded by Lt. William Wheeler, the battery hurried at double-quick to Cemetery Hill on July 1, and then moved forward to support Dilger's battery with its rifled guns. Wheeler recalled watching a shot take off an infantryman's leg, which "whirled like a stone through the air, until it came against a caisson with a loud whack."

Dedicated in 1893
39.84253, -77.232961; see map C

591. 15th and 50th New York Engineer Regiments

The engineer regiments were not at Gettysburg, but they did build bridges for the army to use during the Pennsylvania campaign. Most of the 15th New York Engineers was mustered out at the end of June, leaving behind three companies of three-year men. The monument was designed to look like the castle symbol of the Army Corps of Engineers.

Dedicated in 1889
39.808076, -77.233269; see map W

511. 15th New York Independent Battery (Hart's Battery)

Under the command of Capt. Patrick Hart, the 15th New York Independent Battery dueled with enemy artillery until Joseph Kershaw's South Carolinians attacked. "This attack was repulsed by the battery; the enemy formed for a second charge and were repulsed again. But the battery having exhausted its stock of canister, and having nothing left in the caissons except some solid shot, was obliged to withdraw."

Dedicated in 1888
39.801001, -77.248181; see map V

621. 39th New York Infantry (Garibaldi Guards)

The 39th New York's main monument is in Ziegler's Grove. This smaller marker indicates where the regiment recaptured Union artillery on July 2. Wrote one soldier, "[W]e went into it with such a yell and scream that it made my blood chill in my veins. I can't tell you how the shot and shell flew. Oh! what a sight! to see the men fall one after another. But the groans were drowned by our shouts."

39.802918, -77.23789; see map W

216. 39th New York Infantry (Garibaldi Guards)

The 39th New York was a polyglot regiment, with Hungarian, Italian, Swiss, French, Spanish, and Portuguese companies. On July 3, it fought "valiantly," said a state history. "Three battle flags were captured by the 39th, a Mass. battery was recaptured, and the regiment received official commendation for its valor." A second marker north of United States Avenue indicates where the regiment supported the 3rd Corps on July 2.

Dedicated in 1888
39.814158, -77.235281; see map M

UNION CORPS BADGES AT GETTYSBURG

After Maj. Gen. Joseph Hooker took command of the Army of the Potomac in January 1863, he had his chief of staff, Daniel Butterfield, design distinctive badges for each of the army's corps. These corps badges are often worked into monument designs.

1st Corps: Circle	6th Corps: Cross
2nd Corps: Trefoil	11th Corps: Crescent
3rd Corps: Diamond	12th Corps: Star
5th Corps: Maltese Cross	

759. 40th New York Infantry (Mozart Regiment, United States Constitution Guard)

On July 2, the 40th New York reached Devil's Den. "Here we push in, the fighting being very hot, with the rebels not more than twenty paces off and outnumbering us three to one," said Lt. Joseph Murphy. "But we held Hood's veterans in check long enough to enable Vincent's Brigade to occupy and save the all-important position on Little Round Top." The unit got its name from New York City's Mozart Hall Committee.

Dedicated in 1888
39.792417, -77.24048; see map BB

247. 41st New York Infantry (De Kalb Regiment)

The German 41st New York belonged to the brigade of Leopold von Gilsa, its first colonel. It called itself the De Kalb regiment, adopting the name from Company A, which predated the war. The regiment did not arrive at Gettysburg until 10:00 pm on July 1; it assembled on Cemetery Hill, where it participated in the fighting on July 2 and 3. It suffered 76 men killed or wounded.

Dedicated in 1893
39.821326, -77.227288; see map N

CASUALTIES AT GETTYSBURG

Gettysburg was the bloodiest battle of the entire Civil War. The Army of Northern Virginia suffered 4,708 killed, 12,693 wounded, and an additional 5,830 captured or missing. Union losses were 3,155 killed, 14,530 wounded, and 5,369 missing or captured.

547. 42ⁿᵈ New York Infantry (Tammany Regiment)

The 42ⁿᵈ New York was not a Native American regiment, its monument notwithstanding. It was raised by the Tammany Society, a political group in New York City that used the Delaware chief as its symbol. At Gettysburg, the regiment suffered 74 casualties among its 197 men. Its colonel was James E. Mallon. The color bearer, Sgt. Michael Cuddy was killed. "When he fell, mortally wounded, he rose by a convulsive effort, and triumphantly waved in the face of the rebels, not 10 yards distant, that flag he loved so dearly, of which he was so proud, and for which his valuable life, without a murmur, was freely given up," reported Mallon.

39.812065, -77.235468; see map W

644. 43ʳᵈ New York Infantry

The 43ʳᵈ New York participated in the 6ᵗʰ Corps' 36-mile forced march to reach Gettysburg and then was posted on this spot to operate in reserve. On July 3, it and the rest of Neill's brigade attacked skirmishers on the Confederate left. "The loss of the Forty-third at Gettysburg was small compared with most battles in which it took part with the Army of the Potomac," read a regimental history.

Dedicated in 1889
39.807892, -77.210237; see map Z

"It was a grand battle, and in my judgment a most decided victory, though I did not bag or annihilate the Confederate army . . . . The men behaved splendidly; I really think they are becoming soldiers."

—Maj. Gen. George Meade in a letter to his wife
written on July 5

808. 44th and 12th New York Infantry

With Strong Vincent mortally wounded, Col. James C. Rice of the 44th New York assumed brigade command. The Confederates "tried for an hour in vain to break the lines of the Forty-fourth New York and Eighty-third Pennsylvania, charging again and again within a few yards of those unflinching troops," Rice recalled. Daniel Butterfield, who once commanded the 12th New York and served as Meade's chief of staff at Gettysburg, designed this monument.

Dedicated in 1893–1900
39.791276, -77.236988; see map CC

45. 45th New York Infantry (5th German Rifles)

The 45th New York was a German regiment from New York City. Its colonel was George von Amsberg, a veteran of the 1848 Hungarian Revolution who was boosted to brigade command on July 1. Regimental skirmishers captured Confederates at the McLean barn— one of the captives turned out be the brother of the 45th's Cpl. Rudolph Schwartz, who was killed soon afterwards. The Confederates captured many from the regiment during the retreat through town.

Dedicated in 1888
39.840649, -77.234726; see map C

40. 45th New York Infantry (5th German Rifles)

The 45th New York was part of the 1th Corps and moved as far as this spot on the first day's fighting. The regiment's main monument is on Howard Avenue.

39.844457, -77.240042; see map C

636. 49th New York Infantry

Positioned with its brigade at the far right of the Army of Potomac's line of infantry, the 49th New York served in a reserve capacity. On July 3, the regiment "made a vigorous and successful attack on the skirmish line of Johnson's Division, which was protecting the extreme left of Lee's army."

Dedicated in 1893
39.807609, -77.211496; see map Y

693. 52nd New York Infantry (German Rangers, Sigel Rifles)

On July 2, the 52nd New York moved forward to support the 3rd Corps in the Wheatfield. "Here the regiment, together with the brigade, commenced firing, giving the enemy, who was about 100 yards in front of our line, three or four good volleys," according to Capt. William Scherrer. The federals pushed the rebels out, but then retreated to keep from being outflanked.

Dedicated in 1893
39.797448, -77.245364; see map BB

69. 54th New York Infantry (Hiram Barney Rifles)

On July 1, the 54th New York held the extreme right of Francis Barlow's division, with its right resting on Rock Creek. Like the rest of the 11th Corps, it was forced to retreat to Cemetery Hill. The regiment's main monument is on Wainwright Avenue.

39.845896, -77.224181; see map D

226. 54th New York Infantry (Hiram Barney Rifles)

One of the German regiments that characterized the 11th Corps, the 54th New York fell back during the Confederate assault on the evening of July 2. One of the first to die was its color bearer, Sgt. Henry Michel. Once reinforcements arrived, the regiment "made a stand, assumed the aggressive and took part in a hand-to-hand fight, finally driving back the enemy and taking up again its old position," said a 1902 history.

Dedicated in 1890
39.822176, -77.227826; see map N

701. 57th New York Infantry

The 57th New York was one of the 2nd Corps regiments sent to aid the 3rd Corps on July 2. They received the order to move around 4:00 pm. "As we pushed forward a bullet struck my right arm and passed through it," recalled the regiment's Jacob Henry Cole. "As we charged the wheatfield a shell exploded and shattered my right leg and killed two of my comrades."

Dedicated in 1889
39.796792, -77.244632; see map BB

61. 58th New York Infantry

The 58th New York had about 50 men on the field on July 1. "As nearly the whole number of our regiment had been on picket duty and on the reconnaissance with me, and I had not been able to find the brigade, it could take but little part in the fight of July 1," reported Capt. Emil Koenig, who took command when Lt. Col. August Otto assumed a staff position with Maj. Gen. Carl Schurz. The monument still bears scars from a lightning strike in the 1930s.

Dedicated in 1888
39.843728, -77.228092; see map D

546. 59th New York Infantry

Losses had reduced the 59th New York to only 120 men, so it had been reorganized into a battalion of four companies just days before the battle. During Pickett's Charge, the regiment battled the 48th Georgia. Sgt. James Wiley received the Medal of Honor for capturing the Georgia regiment's flag.

Dedicated in 1889
39.812099, -77.236136; see map W

326. 60th New York Infantry (Union Guards)

The 60th New York was part of George Greene's brigade, left to defend Culp's Hill when the rest of the 12th Corps moved to support the Union left. On the evening of July 2, "Four separate and distinct charges were made on our line before 9:30 o'clock, which were effectually resisted." Fighting resumed in the morning. "During this attack the fire was kept up constantly and effectively along the whole line."

Dedicated in 1889
39.819746, -77.219564; see map O

327. 60th New York Infantry, Company I

The 60th New York fended off serious attacks on the evening of July 2. "If ever men loaded and fired more rapidly than the 60th did on that occasion, I never saw them do it," recalled one soldier. This marker indicates the advanced position of its Company I.

39.819457, -77.21935; see map O

721. 61st New York Infantry (Clinton Guards)

The 61st New York participated in the desperate fighting in the Wheatfield on July 2 under Lt. Col. K. Oscar Broady. "The wounds received by my men seemed to be of an unusually severe character, and it is to be feared that the greater portion of the wounded will never be fit for active service again," Broady reported.

Dedicated in 1889
39.796993, -77.242012; see map BB

768. 62nd New York Infantry

The 62nd New York reached the battlefield on July 2 and received orders to support the Pennsylvania Reserves. "After delivering several volleys, we charged the enemy's columns, broke them, drove them in disorder down the hill, and captured two light twelve-pounder guns, which had been lost by the Fifth Corps earlier in the day." The capture of the cannon is depicted on the monument's bas-relief.

Dedicated in 1888
39.797156, -77.237323; see map CC

717. 64th New York Infantry

The 64th New York served with Col. John Brooke's 2nd Corps brigade in support of the 3rd Corps on July 2. In the Wheatfield, "The men were firing as fast as they could load," recalled Col. Daniel Bingham. "The din was almost deafening." The fresh troops of the 2nd Corps pushed the enemy back into Rose Woods but before long had to retreat in turn.

Dedicated in 1890
39.794895, -77.247082; see map BB

335. 65th New York Infantry (1st United States Chasseurs)

The 65th New York, also known as the 1st United States Chasseurs, was commanded by Col. Joseph Eldridge Hamblin at Gettysburg. On July 2, it reached the field where its monument now stands; during the battle, it served mainly in a supporting role.

Dedicated in 1889
39.817986, -77.219604; see map O

697. 66th New York Infantry (Governor's Guard)

According to a regimental history of the 66th New York, "Most of the loss was met in the Wheatfield, and the road just beyond. Colonel Morris and Lieutenant Colonel Hammell were both wounded. Capt. George H. Ince was killed, and Lieutenant Banta shot through the lungs." The monument stands at the point of the regiment's farthest advance.

Dedicated in 1889
39.79723, -77.245073; see map BB

342. 67th New York Infantry (1st Long Island Volunteers)

According to Lt. Col. H. L. Van Ness, the 67th New York was "in all parts of the field" during the three days of fighting. Early on July 3, the regiment was sent to the Union right and "drove the enemy from the Rifle pits, and occupied them for three hours when we were relieved."

Dedicated in 1888
39.817527, -77.219721; see map O

235. 68th New York Infantry (Cameron Rifles, 2nd German Rifle Regiment)

Like the 54th New York, the 68th New York broke and retreated during Jubal Early's dusk attack on July 2. Reinforced, it turned and resisted, sometimes hand to hand. A German regiment, it had originally been called the Cameron Rifles, after then-secretary of war Simon Cameron, as well as the 2nd German Rifle Regiment.

Dedicated in 1888
39.82191, -77.227654; see map N

503. 73rd New York (4th Excelsior, 2nd Fire Zouaves)

With its core formed by New York City firefighters, the 73rd New York was also known as the 2nd Fire Zouaves (and the 4th Excelsior for its position in the Excelsior Brigade). In fierce fighting on July 2, Barksdale's Mississippians drove the 73rd New York back, the rebels "firing and shrieking like Indians."

Dedicated in 1897
39.802126, -77.248148; see map V

38. 76th New York Infantry

The corps badge for the 1st Corps was a circle, which explains the circle atop the 76th New York Infantry's monument. The monument also includes the New York state seal in bronze. "At Gettysburg the regiment took a prominent part and suffered the loss of 234 in killed, wounded and missing," read a New York history.

Dedicated in 1888
39.83994, -77.246793; see map B

319. 76th New York Infantry

The main monument of the 76th New York is on Reynolds Avenue, where the regiment fought on July 1. This marker indicates its location on July 2 and 3.

39.820176, -77.22015; see map O

640. 77th New York Infantry

The 77th New York was posted on Power's Hill, the headquarters of Maj. Gen. Henry Slocum of the 12th Corps. "At Gettysburg it was not closely engaged and proceeded from that battlefield to Fairfield, Pa., Antietam, Marsh Run, Funks-town, Williamsport and Chantilly," read a 1908 history.

Dedicated in 1889
39.805401, -77.219348; see map Y

333. 78th and 102nd New York Infantry

On the evening of July 2, the 78th New York resisted advancing Confederates, "and as the shadows of evening deepened in the forest defiles of Rock Creek, the flashes from their rifles glowed with an angry light," said a 1902 history. The regiment moved back to a spot next to the 102nd New York, "and at 9:30 pm the discomfited enemy withdrew to await daylight before attempting further efforts." Fighting resumed at 3:30 the next morning.

Dedicated in 1888
39.818479, -77.219565; see map O

123. 80th New York Infantry (20th New York State Militia; Ulster Guard)

As the Confederates outflanked the regiments of the Union's 1st Corps on July 1, first the 121st Pennsylvania and then the 80th New York were forced to withdraw back toward Seminary Ridge.

Dedicated in 1888
39.831442, -77.251299; see map G

562. 80th New York Infantry (20th New York State Militia; Ulster Guard)

Raised mostly from New York's Ulster County, the 80th New York Infantry has its main monument on Doubleday Avenue. This marker indicates its position on July 3, when it was able to fire into the advancing Confederates' flanks. Its colonel, Theodore B. Gates, also had responsibility for the 151st Pennsylvania.

Dedicated in 1888
39.810293, -77.236086; see map W

561. 82nd New York Infantry

Under command of Col. James Huston, the 82nd New York advanced to support the 3rd Corps on July 2. On July 3, it participated in the repulse of Pickett's Charge near the Copse of Trees. "The regiment was conspicuous for its dash and daring and became famous for its fighting qualities," read a 1908 history of the Civil War.

Dedicated in 1890
39.810373, -77.236074; see map W

27. 83rd New York Infantry (9th Regiment New York State Militia)

The 83rd New York was under the command of Lt. Col. Joseph A. Moesch, who had been born in Switzerland. On July 1, as the Confederates of Iverson's brigade approached, the New Yorkers "displayed great coolness, reserving their fire until the enemy came within fifty yards, when a murderous volley was poured into their ranks, which sent them reeling back in utter confusion, followed closely by the brigade, whose cheers rent the air."

Dedicated in 1888
39.84297, -77.242442; see map B

104. 84th New York (14th Brooklyn) Infantry

Also known as the 14th Brooklyn, this tested regiment of brightly garbed "red-legged devils" fought under the command of Col. Edward D. Fowler. The regiment fought alongside the 6th Wisconsin and the 95th New York for the railroad cut, where they killed and captured the Mississippians of Davis's brigade.

Dedicated in 1887
39.837577, -77.248285; see map G

89. 84th New York (14th Brooklyn) Infantry

The 84th New York opened their fighting on July 1 near here before moving to their right and rear to charge the railroad cut, where the regiment's main monument is located.

Dedicated in 1893
39.835751, -77.253011; see map G

348. 84th New York Infantry
(14th Brooklyn)

The main monument to the 14th Brooklyn (84th New York) is on Reynolds Avenue, where the regiment fought on July 1. This marker indicates where the regiment encountered the advance rebels of Johnson's division on the night of July 2. Col. Edward Fowler recollected that this surprise encounter with the rebels so near the Union artillery reserve "was of very great importance."

39.817076, -77.219574; see map O

751. 86th New York Infantry

On the afternoon of July 2, the 86th New York faced advancing rebels, "but our ranks pouring out a deadly fire checked them, and they were driven back," said Maj. Samuel H. Leavitt. "Rallying again they reformed and fired a sharp volley at us which caused our line to waver some, but we hung on grimly and maintained our ground until 5 p.m." Then the 86th New York was forced to retreat.

Dedicated in 1888
39.793639, -77.242699; see map BB

302. 93rd New York Infantry

This New York Infantry regiment had fought during the Seven Days' Battles in Virginia, but after that was assigned to headquarters guard duty, a post it still held during the Gettysburg battle.

Dedicated in 1890
39.814602, -77.231975; see map N

36. 94th New York Infantry

The 94th New York reached this position on the afternoon of July 1. "The Ninety-fourth assisted here in repelling several strong attacks, during which a large number of Confederate prisoners were captured and several battle flags taken," said a history of New York regiments. "Eighty-one dead Confederates were counted the following day, lying in front of the Ninety-fourth's position."

Dedicated in 1888
39.841201, -77.242899; see map B

105. 95th New York Infantry

Led by Maj. Edward Pye after the wounding of Col. George H. Biddle, the 95th New York supported the 6th Wisconsin's charge on the railroad cut on July 1. "Colonel Biddle, of the Ninety-fifth, was wounded early in the fight and retired from the field, the command devolving then on Maj. Edward Pye," read a history. "My regiment behaved very well, and gave me just cause to be proud of it," Pye reported. "All the officers, with one or two exceptions, behaved well."

Dedicated in 1893
39.837441, -77.248125; see map G

37. 95th New York Infantry

This small marker on Doubleday Avenue indicates the position the 95th New York Infantry held around noon on July 1.

39.839481, -77.243976; see map B

129. 95th New York Infantry

This marker on the corner of Seminary Ridge Road and Chambersburg Pike indicates the position the 95th New York held when it fell back during the fighting on July 2.

39.834501, –77.244665; see map H

320. 95th New York

This position marker on Culp's Hill indicates the 95th New York's location on July 2 and 3.

39.820217, –77.220027; see map O

31. 97th New York Infantry (Conkling Rifles)

The 97th New York, firing from behind a stone wall, participated in the rout of Iverson's brigade on July 1. "Boys of the 97th, let us go for them and capture them," shouted Lt. Col. John P. Spofford when he observed the stricken rebels. Col. Charles Wheelock later got into a dispute with his brigade commander when he refused to send a captured flag to the rear. Wheelock was taken prisoner during the retreat through Gettysburg, but he escaped and rejoined the regiment.

Dedicated in 1889
39.842426, –77.242465; see map B

26. 104th New York Infantry (Wadsworth Guards)

As part of the 1st Brigade of the 2nd Division in the 1st Corps, the 104th New York experienced heavy fighting on July 1 under Col. Gilbert G. Prey. One officer, Capt. George H. Starr, was captured and escaped from three different Confederate prisons before he made it back to Union lines in 1864.

Dedicated in 1888
39.843309, -77.241735; see map B

369. 107th New York Infantry

Read a 1908 history, "The regiment was only slightly engaged at Gettysburg, and after the battle joined with its corps in pursuit of Lee into Virginia, engaging without loss at Jones' cross-roads and near Williamsport, Md."

Dedicated in 1888
39.814733, -77.216702; see map O

285. 108th New York Infantry (Rochester Regiment)

Called the Rochester Regiment after the city where it was raised, the 108th New York served in the 2nd Corps, which had a trefoil, or cloverleaf, as its badge. On July 3, the regiment withstood the Confederate artillery barrage from here. One soldier said it was "perfectly awful, murderous." The regiment got its revenge when its fire helped repulse the Confederate advance.

Dedicated in 1888
39.816229, -77.234638; see map N

205. 111th New York Infantry

The 111th New York was among the units who surrendered at Harpers Ferry in September 1862 and were taunted as "Harpers Ferry Cowards" since. As the New Yorkers charged forward to repulse Gen. James Barksdale's Mississippians on July 2, they shouted, "Remember Harpers Ferry!" On July 3, they repulsed more Mississippi troops from this position near the Brian farm. "Not a man flinched, but every brow was knit and lip compressed with stern determination to win or die, and win they did," reported Capt. Aaron P. Seeley.

Dedicated in 1891
39.815405, -77.23547; see map M

56. 119th New York Infantry

Col. John T. Lockman took over the 119th New York after its commander was killed at Chancellorsville. At Gettysburg, the regiment "was heavily engaged on the first two days of the battle, losing 140 in killed, wounded and missing," according to a 1908 history.

Dedicated in 1888
39.843083, -77.230836; see map C

495. 120th New York Infantry

As Barksdale's Mississippians approached, the 120th New York lay on the ground, waiting for the order to rise and fire; then "the whole line rose as a man and poured into their ranks such a terrible fire of musketry, as to bring them to a standstill when within a few rods of us," recalled one soldier.

Dedicated in 1889
39.804691, -77.24608; see map V

796. 121ˢᵗ New York Infantry

Col. Emory Upton, who commanded the 121ˢᵗ New York, would go on to greater rank and fame during the 1864 Overland Campaign. Reaching here late on July 2, his regiment remained in reserve. The statue that once stood atop the pedestal was removed for repair after being hit by a falling tree limb.

39.793602, -77.235448; see map CC

338. 122ⁿᵈ New York Infantry (3ʳᵈ Onondaga Regiment)

James M. Gere of the 122ⁿᵈ New York wrote that early on July 3, the regiment fought a "tempest of rebel attack—firing for three hours and a half—smiting and destroying its strength till what remained of the rebel force that could get away, riven and torn, drifted back over the hill: the right of our position was restored and the field was yet in condition to be finally won."

Dedicated in 1888
39.817867, -77.219481; see map O

357. 123ʳᵈ New York Infantry

Early on July 3, the 123ʳᵈ New York, commanded by Lt. Col. James C. Rogers, received orders to relieve the 20ᵗʰ Connecticut, which was driving Confederates from works they had occupied. In his report, Rogers said, "the enemy having been driven from the breastworks," the regiment "moved forward and occupied them."

Dedicated in 1888
39.816017, -77.217901; see map O

356. 123rd New York Infantry

When its brigade commander ordered the 123rd New York to regain works captured by the rebels, he said he hoped to see them "master of the works." Recalled a soldier, "The Colonel's hopes were realized; for the works were immediately charged and gained without serious loss." The regiment's main monument is nearby.

39.816248, -77.217206; see map O

753. 124th New York Infantry (Orange Blossoms)

As the 1st Texas Infantry approached the 124th New York at Devil's Den on July 2, "marching as if on parade, across the open field," Lt. Col. Augustus van Horne Ellis ordered his men to stand and fire. The Texans fell back, and the New Yorkers charged. "In this charge we suffered severely," said Lt. Col. Francis M. Cummins. Ellis was among the dead. "He was one of those dashing and chivalrous spirits that we frequently read of, but seldom encounter in real life," noted Brig. Gen. J. H. Hobart Ward.

Dedicated in 1884
39.79277, -77.242695; see map BB

575. 124th New York Infantry

Recruited in Orange County, New York, the 124th New York became known as the Orange Blossoms and fought at Devil's Den on July 2. This marker indicates the regiment's position on July 3, but it did not participate in the repulse of the Confederate attack on that day. The 124th's main monument is at Devil's Den.

39.808637, -77.235267; see map W

212. 125th New York Infantry

The regiment's original commander, Col. George L. Willard, was killed while holding brigade command on July 2. Col. Levin Crandall commanded the regiment, which repulsed the Confederate attack on July 3 from behind a stone wall here. The trefoil, or cloverleaf, atop the 125th New York's monument reflects the badge of the 2nd Corps, to which it belonged. Many of the regimental monuments similarly incorporate their corps badges.

Dedicated in 1888
39.814728, -77.235277; see map M

284. 126th New York Infantry

The 126th New York, like the 111th, was one of the regiments castigated as "Harpers Ferry Cowards." During the cannonade on July 3, the men moved into Ziegler's Grove to find some protection. When the shelling ended they moved forward to aid in the rebel repulse. The bas-relief is of Col. Eliakim Sherrill, advanced to brigade command on July 2 and temporarily arrested by Hancock for ordering a withdrawal. Sherrill was killed in the fighting on July 3.

Dedicate in 1888
39.816689, -77.234521; see map N

225. 134th New York Infantry

The 134th New York saw the worst of its fighting on July 1 when, as part of Col. Charles Coster's brigade, it went forward to support the collapsing Union defenses and suffered devastating losses. "I never imagined such a rain of bullets," said one officer. Crowned by a minie ball, the monument indicates the regiment's position on July 2, when it helped defend East Cemetery Hill against the men of Jubal Early's division.

Dedicated in 1888
39.822085, -77.229454; see map N

151. 134th New York Infantry

With Col. Charles R. Coster (for whom Coster Avenue is named) promoted to brigade command, Lt. Col. Allan H. Jackson led the 134th New York when it covered the retreat of the 11th Corps through Gettysburg. In the fight, "the brigade sustained a terrible loss, more than half its men being shot down at this place. The remnant of the regiment then made its escape, and returned to Cemetery Hill."

39.835258, -77.227147; see map J

269. 136th New York Infantry

Under Colonel James Wood Jr., the 136th New York reached Cemetery Hill with the rest of its brigade on July 1 as the 1st and 11th Corps were falling back. The "skirmishing and sharpshooting was so active and continuous that the regiment, without participating in any other fighting, lost 106 men killed and wounded."

Dedicated in 1888
39.819154, -77.232921; see map N

345. 137th New York Infantry

The 137th New York was in the thick of the confused fighting in the darkness on the night of July 2, as men from Early's division moved into the breastworks left empty when the rest of Geary's division left for the Union left. Commanded by Col. David Ireland, the 137th New York had the greatest casualties of any regiment in its brigade.

Dedicated in 1889
39.817395, -77.219658; see map O

807. 140th New York Infantry

The bronze likeness on the 140th New York's monument is of Col. Patrick O'Rorke, the regiment's commander. When Gouverneur Warren sought more men to defend Little Round Top on July 2, he found O'Rorke, who ordered his men move at double-quick up the rocks. He started to align his men but Warren stopped him. There was no time. "Take your men immediately into action." O'Rorke did and went straight to his death.

Dedicated in 1889
39.79139, -77.237266; see map CC

363. 145th New York Infantry (Stanton Legion)

The 145th New York left Culp's Hill to support the Union left and upon returning received fire from Confederates occupying their former breastworks, which created a "near approach to a panic," according to the brigade commander. "At daylight, on the 3d," read a 1902 history, "the regiment assisted in driving out the enemy, and reoccupied its line about 11 o'clock, am, losing 1 killed and 9 wounded, of whom 2 subsequently died of their wounds and were buried in the cemetery at Gettysburg."

Dedicated in 1890
39.815415, -77.217317; see map O

799. 146th New York Infantry

Part of Steven Weed's brigade, the 146th New York reached Little Round Top just in time on July 2. "Hood's Division of Longstreet's Corps were just climbing the hill when we reached the top and in a hand-to-hand encounter drove them back," remembered one officer.

Dedicated in 1880
39.792731, -77.236731; see map CC

102. 147th New York Infantry

Part of Brig. Gen. Lysander Cutler's 2nd Brigade of the 1st Corps' 1st Division at Gettysburg, the 147th New York was organized in Oswego, New York. On July 1, they advanced toward the railroad cut. "Men began to fall on all sides before we fired a shot," remembered J. Volnay Pierce of Company G. The regiment also fought on Culp's Hill on July 2 and 3.

Dedicated in 1888
39.838072, -77.247837; see map G

340. 147th New York Infantry

The 147th New York's primary monument is on Reynolds Avenue, where the regiment fought for the railroad cut on July 1 before falling back to this position on Culp's Hill to experience two more days of battle and death.

39.81807, -77.219044; see map O

339. 149th New York Infantry

The bas-relief on the 149th New York's monument is based on "Mending the Flag" by Edwin Forbes, which depicts Sgt. William Lilly repairing the staff during the fighting here. In the words of a 1908 history, "At Gettysburg the regiment participated in the famous defense of Culp's hill, made by Greene's brigade, in which the 149th, fighting behind breastworks, lost 6 killed, 46 wounded and 3 missing, but inflicted many times that loss on its assailants."

Dedicated in 1892
39.817944, -77.219324; see map O

329. 150th New York Infantry
(The Duchess County Regiment)

The 150th New York was untested in battle when it reached Gettysburg. According to one account, a brigadier general approached Col. John Ketcham and warned him that his green regiment might need support. "Contrary to the expectations of the Brigadier General our boys fought like devils," said a newspaper account. When told it was the green regiment, the general exclaimed, "Well I wish to God they were all green."

Dedicated in 1889
39.819107, -77.219657; see map O

520. 150th New York Infantry

This marker commemorates the action of the 150th New York on July 2 when it recaptured guns the Mississippians of Barksdale's brigade had captured from the 9th Massachusetts (Bigelow's) battery.

39.801667, -77.242479; see map V

150. 154th New York Infantry

One of the men of the 154th New York who fought a rearguard action in the brickyard here was Sgt. Amos Humiston. He died that day, the only clue to his identity an ambrotype of three children clutched in his hand. He was identified that November, when his widow read a story about the unknown soldier and his photograph. Interest spurred by the story led to the founding of Gettysburg's National Soldiers' Orphan Homestead in 1866.

Dedicated in 1890
39.835165, -77.227565; see map I

42. 157th New York Infantry

As the Union line collapsed on July 1, the 157th New York attacked Doles's brigade. The Union troops suffered terribly, with 75 percent losses. This is one of two monuments and a marker to the regiment. The second monument is farther down Howard Avenue at the corner of Carlisle Road.

Dedicated in 1886
39.840123, -77.236532; see map C

55. 157th New York Infantry

This is the second monument to the 157th New York on Howard Avenue. The regiment suffered terrible casualties in its fight with the Confederates of Doles's brigade here on July 1. The crescent moon on the monument is the badge of the 11th Corps and is visible on many monuments here.

Dedicated in 1886
39.84304, -77.231346; see map C

41. 157th New York

The 157th New York has two monuments on Howard Avenue. This position marker indicates how far forward it advanced on July 1.

39.845585, -77.231383; see map C

504. Excelsior Brigade (70–74th New York Infantry)

Former congressman Daniel Sickles raised the regiments of the Excelsior Brigade and led them in battle before being promoted to command of the 3rd Corps. According to legend, a bust of Sickles was to occupy the center of the monument. That plan ended when the 93-year-old ex-general was arrested in 1913 because more than $28,000 had gone missing from the state monument commission for which he served as chairman. Sickles still has no statue on the battlefield.

Dedicated in 1893
39.801783, -77.247505; see map V

700. Irish Brigade (63rd, 69th and 88th New York)

The Irish Brigade was the 2nd Brigade of the 2nd Corps' 1st Division and, along with the regiments listed on its monument, also included the 28th Massachusetts and the 116th Pennsylvania. The monument's Celtic cross underscores the brigade's dominant nationality. Hard fighting in earlier battles had greatly reduced the brigade's numbers—at Gettysburg it was down to only 530 out of its original 2,500. The Irish wolfhound is a symbol of loyalty.

Dedicated in 1888
39.797056, -77.245155; see map BB

ARTILLERY AT GETTYSBURG

There were 631 cannon present during the battle. Cannon came in two basic types: rifled and smoothbore. Armies tended to use the more accurate rifled guns (such as the 3-inch ordnance rifle) to knock out enemy artillery. Smoothbores—including the 10-pound Parrott gun, recognizable by the iron reinforcing band wrapped around the breech—were most often used against soldiers. Another smoothbore, the 12-pound Napoleon, was made of bronze; the copper makes these guns turn green.

435. New York Sharpshooters (1st Regiment United States Sharpshooters, Companies A, B, D & H)

On the afternoon of July 2, the four companies of the 1st United States Sharpshooters (four from New York and one from Vermont) pushed forward across the Emmitsburg Road on a scouting mission. There they became involved in a firefight with Wilcox's Alabamians—a development that helped persuade Daniel Sickles that he should move his 3rd Corps forward.

Dedicated in 1889
39.808058, -77.257612; see map U

615. New York State Auxiliary Monument

Almost 475,000 New Yorkers joined the Union forces during the war, the largest contribution of any state. Some 50,000 of them died. This monument lists the regiments from the Empire State that fought at Gettysburg, as well as the commanders who have statues elsewhere on the battlefield. There's also a list of those who don't—including Daniel Sickles, the only Union corps commander not so honored.

Dedicated in 1889
39.804096, -77.234459; see map W

248. New York State Monument

Based on Trajan's Column in Rome, the New York State Monument faces the state's section in the National Cemetery. It is 93 feet high. The statue at the top is 13 feet tall. It was dedicated on July 3, 1893, and cost 59,095 dollars and 3 cents. New York contributed almost 475,000 soldiers to the Union army, more than any other state.

Dedicated in 1893
39.820789, -77.230596; see map N

299. Oneida New York Cavalry

Attached to the army headquarters, the 49 men of this cavalry regiment served to protect headquarters and deliver messages around the battlefield.

Dedicated in 1904
39.814543, -77.232276; see map N

NORTH CAROLINA

95. 26th North Carolina Infantry

Commanded by 21-year-old Col. Henry Burgwyn Jr., who was born in Massachusetts but spent much of his youth in North Carolina, the 26th North Carolina engaged in a furious battle with the 24th Michigan here on July 1. Burgwyn fell mortally wounded as his regiment forced the federals back. The regiment has another monument on Cemetery Ridge.

Dedicated in 1985
39.834715, -77.254606; see map G

522. 26th North Carolina Infantry

The 26th North Carolina belonged to Pettigrew's brigade in Pender's division of A. P. Hill's corps. It had the unfortunate distinction of having the highest casualty rate—82 percent—of any regiment at Gettysburg. The marker here commemorates the regiment's participation in the attack on July 3—Pickett's Charge. By the time they reached this point, the regiment "had been reduced to a skirmish line." Another monument on Meredith Avenue marks where the regiment fought on July 1.

Dedicated in 1986
39.813539, -77.235543; see map W

310. 43rd North Carolina Infantry

The 43rd North Carolina fought hard on July 1, but this monument recalls their fighting on the morning of July 3. The regiment, part of Daniel's brigade, attacked the federal trenches at the base of Culp's Hill and even managed to capture a portion before being forced to withdraw.

Dedicated in 1988
39.818665, -77.215517; see map O

189. North Carolina State Monument

The sculptor of the North Carolina State Monument was Gutzon Borglum, best known today for Mt. Rushmore. The bronze casting for the monument was done in New York. North Carolina seceded from the Union on May 20, 1861, following Lincoln's request for troops to put down the rebellion. Up to 125,000 North Carolinians fought for the Confederacy, and they accounted for around a quarter of the Confederate losses during the war.

Dedicated in 1929
39.81839, -77.247499; see map L

OHIO

597. 1st Ohio Cavalry, Companies A&C

Companies A and C of the 1st Ohio Cavalry were assigned to headquarters during the battle.

Dedicated in 1887
39.808309, -77.230627; see map W

273. 1st Ohio Light Artillery, Battery H (Huntington's Battery)

Part of the Artillery Reserve, Battery H of the 1st Ohio Light Artillery was ordered into action to replace a battery and remained there until the fighting ended. Its commander was Lt. George Norton, who reported firing a total of 767 rounds over July 2 and 3.

Dedicated in 1887
39.81823, -77.231507; see map N

49. 1st Ohio Light Artillery, Battery I (Dilger's Battery)

Commanded by Capt. Hubert Dilger, Battery I of the 1st Ohio Light Artillery had six Napoleons, which it used in "a heavy artillery duel" on July 1. The battery also fired canister at advancing Confederates over the heads of skirmishers of the 45th New York.

Dedicated in 1887
39.841865, -77.23389; see map C

147. 1st Ohio Light Artillery, Battery K (Heckman's Battery)

Under the command of Capt. Lewis Heckman, the 1st Ohio Light Artillery's Battery K helped cover the 11th Corps' retreat on July 1. "In the battle of Gettysburg the battery was so closely engaged as to lose five men killed and twenty-seven wounded," read an Ohio history.

Dedicated in 1887
39.836982, -77.231335; see map I

794. 1ˢᵗ Ohio Artillery, Battery L (Gibbs's Battery)

Battery L, 1ˢᵗ Ohio Artillery, commanded by Capt. Frank C. Gibbs, followed the 5ᵗʰ Corps "on the trot" to Little Round Top on July 2. "So close was the work that the guns were double-shotted with canister, and worked so rapidly that the men could not lay hands upon them. The battery became the nucleus around which the hotly-pressed division rallied and forced the enemy back to his lines."

Dedicated in 1887
39.793596, –77.236355; see map CC

257. 4ᵗʰ Ohio Infantry

Sent by Gen. Hancock to support the defense of East Cemetery Hill, the 4ᵗʰ Ohio of Col. Samuel Carroll's brigade rushed into action on the evening of July 2. Carroll ordered the brigade to fix bayonets and then to "Give them hell!"

Dedicated in 1887
39.821059, –77.228744; see map N

198. 4ᵗʰ Ohio Infantry, Companies G & I

Two companies of the 4ᵗʰ Ohio advanced to this forward position on the afternoon of July 2. In the evening, they withdrew to Cemetery Hill, where the regiment's main monument stands today.

Dedicated on September 14, 1887
39.816803, –77.236308; see map M

365. 5ᵗʰ Ohio Infantry (Cincinnati Regiment)

In his history of Ohio in the war, Whitlaw Reid wrote that the 5ᵗʰ Ohio on July 2 "did not suffer much until about four pm, when the shells began to fall thickly around, several of the men being wounded while lying on the ground." The regiment moved to the right of the line at sundown and served as pickets until they returned here around midnight.

Dedicated in 1887
39.816318, -77.22019; see map O

600. 6ᵗʰ Ohio Cavalry

The 6ᵗʰ Ohio Cavalry did not actually fight at Gettysburg, having been sent to guard the army's trains in Maryland. But it did see plenty of hard fighting during the pursuit of Robert E. Lee's army after the battle.

Dedicated in 1887
39.807833, -77.230673; see map W

346. 7ᵗʰ Ohio Infantry

At Gettysburg, the 7ᵗʰ Ohio "was ordered from point to point, where and when reinforcements were most needed. Its loss was small, owing to the protection of breastworks, of which it availed itself in the hottest part of the battle." Its losses were one killed and 17 wounded.

Dedicated in 1887
39.81727, -77.219579; see map O

199. 8th Ohio Infantry

The 8th Ohio moved out here on July 2, under the command of Lt. Col. Franklin Sawyer, where it remained in a perfect position to wreak havoc on the advancing Confederates of Pickett's Charge on the next day. First, though, its soldiers had to suffer beneath the artillery barrage unleashed from both sides. Then, as the men of Pettigrew's division advanced before them, the Ohioans fired into their flanks, sowing panic and death.

Dedicated in 1887
39.816032, -77.237014; see map M

64. 25th and 75th Ohio Infantry

Lt. Col. Jeremiah Williams, in command of the 25th Ohio, recalled that his men and the enemy were so close on July 1 that the flag-bearers hit each other with their staffs. Col. Andrew Harris led the 75th Ohio and attempted to check the Confederate advance "at a dreadful cost of life." Harris took brigade command during the retreat. These regiments have another monument on Wainwright Avenue by Cemetery Hill.

Dedicated in 1887
39.845298, -77.226672; see map D

222. 25th and 75th Ohio Infantry

Capt. George Fox took command of the 75th Ohio upon Col. Andrew Harris's promotion to brigade command. On the evening of July 2, the regiments grappled fiercely with Louisiana troops here. "A hand to hand engagement ensued," Fox wrote. "Too much praise cannot be given to the gallant and patriotic soldiers of the 25th and 75th Ohio." The two regiments have another monument on Howard Avenue at the site of their first day's fighting.

Dedicated in 1887
39.823227, -77.228518; see map N

343. 29th Ohio Infantry

The 29th Ohio fought the Confederates of Ewell's division starting early on the morning of July 3. A regimental history reported that "for six hours the musketry was one continued roll, interspersed at intervals by the crash of artillery."

Dedicated in 1887
39.817609, -77.219502; see map O

260. 55th Ohio Infantry

According to Whitlaw Reid's account of Ohio in the war, the 55th Ohio was not directly engaged in the battle, "but the skirmish-line was subject, most of the time, to a severe fire. The Fifty-Fifth lost in this battle about fifty men."

Dedicated in 1887
39.821454, -77.232927; see map N

48. 61st Ohio Infantry

After the 11th Corps broke and retreated, the 61st Ohio was reportedly one of the last regiments to enter Gettysburg on the way south to Cemetery Hill. The regiment's colonel, Stephen J. McGroarty, "was as brave a man as ever marched to the sound of battle," said one of his soldiers.

Dedicated in 1888
39.841568, -77.234015; see map C

321. 66th Ohio Infantry

The 66th Ohio received orders to retake fortifications on Culp's Hill in the predawn darkness of July 3. "In the discharge of the perilous duty assigned to it, the 66th Ohio had the honor of satisfactorily performing as desperate an undertaking as perhaps was ever given to a single regiment," said its commander, Lt. Col. Eugene Powell.

Dedicated in 1887
39.820007, -77.219893; see map O

262. 73rd Ohio Infantry

The 73rd Ohio reached Cemetery Hill on July 1 as the 1st and 11th Corps were falling back. There it was "almost incessantly engaged on the ground in its front. Its losses during the fight amounted to one hundred and forty-three officers and men out of about three hundred," said Whitlaw Reid in *Ohio in the War*.

Dedicated in 1887
39.820489, -77.2327; see map N

57. 82nd Ohio Infantry

According to Col. James C. Robinson, the 82nd Ohio advanced some 150 to 200 yards beyond the site of its monument on July 1 before being forced to withdraw through town. Robinson was badly wounded during the retreat, and Lt. Col. David Thomson took command.

Dedicated in 1887
39.843249, -77.230049; see map D

62. 107th Ohio Infantry

On July 1, the 107th Ohio received an attack from Georgia troops who were "yelling like Indians in making a savage charge." The regiment entered the battle with 434 men, but had only 171 present after they retreated to Cemetery Hill.

Dedicated in 1887
39.844514, -77.227544; see map D

PENNSYLVANIA

535. 1st Pennsylvania Cavalry

The 1st Pennsylvania Cavalry had been in the thick of things during the Battle of Brandy Station at the beginning of Lee's Pennsylvania campaign. At Gettysburg, the regiment, minus one company, served as headquarters escort.

Dedicated in 1890
39.812885, -77.235344; see map W

779. 1st Pennsylvania Cavalry, Company H

The 1st Pennsylvania Cavalry has a larger monument on Hancock Avenue. The marker for Company H stands here because this company was assigned to the 6th Corps' headquarters.

39.797322, -77.234639; see map CC

120. 1st Pennsylvania Light Artillery, Battery B (Cooper's Battery)

Capt. James. H. Cooper and his Battery B of the 1st Pennsylvania Artillery resisted the Confederate advance on July 1 from this spot with four 3-inch guns until forced to withdraw. Their main monument is on Cemetery Hill.

39.832326, -77.251033; see map G

233. 1st Pennsylvania Light Artillery, Battery B (Cooper's Battery)

Capt. James H. Cooper's battery exchanged fire with enemy artillery on Benner's Hill to the northeast for about two and a half hours on July 2, until Ricketts's battery relieved it around 7:00 pm. The battery also has a monument on South Reynolds Avenue, where it fought on July 1, and a tablet on Hancock Avenue, showing its position on July 3.

Dedicated in 1879
39.82175, -77.228676; see map N

244. 1st Pennsylvania Light Artillery, Batteries F and G (Ricketts's Battery)

Under the command of Capt. Robert B. Ricketts, the battery, with six 3-inch ordnance rifles, established a position here. Around 8:00 pm on July 2, "a heavy column of the enemy charged on my battery, and succeeded in capturing and spiking my left piece," Ricketts reported. His men fought hand to hand "with handspikes, rammers, and pistols" until reinforcements helped drive the rebels back.

Dedicated in 1890
39.82145, -77.228677; see map N

724. 1st Pennsylvania Reserves (30th Pennsylvania Infantry)

On July 2, the 1st Pennsylvania Reserves (30th Pennsylvania) reached the field near Little Round Top as the regulars of the 5th Corps were retreating, which was "anything but assuring," in the words of one soldier. Then the regiment "charged the enemy with the most determined spirit, driving him back upon his reserves, and strewing the field with his dead."

Dedicated in 1890
39.796521, –77.240481; see map BB

296. 2nd Pennsylvania Cavalry

Attached to the provost guard of army headquarters, the 2nd Pennsylvania Cavalry suffered no casualties during the battle.

Dedicated in 1889
39.814307, –77.233614; see map N

726. 2nd Pennsylvania Reserves Infantry (31st Pennsylvania Infantry)

Along with the rest of its brigade, the 2nd Pennsylvania Reserves arrived on July 2 in time to stop the Confederate advance at Little Round Top. "Starting forward with a shout, and delivering a solid volley as they went, they crossed the marshy open space in front, cleared the rocky face of the slope beyond and halted not until they reached the stone wall," wrote Samuel Bates.

Dedicated in 1890
39.796309, –77.241254; see map BB

398. 3rd Pennsylvania Cavalry

William E. Miller was with the 3rd Pennsylvania Cavalry in the fighting on July 3 here, and he took responsibility for leaving his position so he could attack the Confederate cavalry. "So sudden and violent was the collision that many of the horses turned end over end and crushed their riders beneath them," he wrote of the fighting here. Miller earned the Medal of Honor for his actions that day.

Dedicated in 1890
39.827342, -77.16259; see map S

410. 3rd Pennsylvania Heavy Artillery

Members of the newly raised 3rd Pennsylvania Heavy Artillery were charged with mutiny after a protest over being defrauded of their bounty money. The matter settled, the unit reached this spot on July 2, where "for the first time we heard the roar of our guns with an enemy in front of them."

Dedicated in 1889
39.818792, -77.173028; see map T

612. 4th Pennsylvania Cavalry

The 4th Pennsylvania Cavalry, under the command of Lt. Col. William E. Doster, arrived on the field on July 2 and supported the artillery, where the horseman were exposed to "a galling fire" until they were relieved.

Dedicated in 1889
39.804783, -77.234483; see map W

835. 5th Pennsylvania Reserves (34th Pennsylvania Infantry)

On July 2, the 5th Pennsylvania Reserve went to support the Union left on Little Round Top, arriving near the end of the fighting there. That evening, it moved with the rest of the 1st Brigade to the summit of Big Round Top, where it helped build defensive breastworks.

Dedicated in 1890
39.786475, -77.239016; see map FF

818. 6th Pennsylvania Cavalry Regiment

The 6th Pennsylvania Cavalry was also called Rush's Lancers, after their commander and the archaic weapons they once carried. Gen. Meade's son, George, was once a member of Rush's Lancers before being assigned to his father's staff.

Dedicated in 1888
39.779583, -77.260665; see map DD

300. 6th Pennsylvania Cavalry Regiment, Companies E & I

This monument honors two companies of the 6th Pennsylvania Cavalry that served during the battle as a headquarters escort. Another monument to the 6th Pennsylvania Cavalry stands on the Emmitsburg Road, south of the battlefield.

39.814613, -77.232116; see map N

682. 6th Pennsylvania Reserves (35th Pennsylvania)

Also known as the 35th Pennsylvania, the 6th Pennsylvania Reserves was assigned to the 5th Corps. It reached the battlefield on July 2 and, around 2:00 pm, made a charge from the vicinity of Little Round Top, "with but small loss."

Dedicated in 1890
39.797787, -77.239715; see map BB

589. 8th Pennsylvania Cavalry

The 8th Pennsylvania Cavalry did not fight at Gettysburg, having been dispatched to Westminster, Maryland, and then to Emmitsburg. On July 4, it joined Kilpatrick's division for the attack on the retreating Confederates at Monterey Pass and throughout Lee's retreat to Virginia.

Dedicated in 1890
39.808305, -77.234683; see map W

812. 9th Pennsylvania Reserves (38th Pennsylvania Infantry)

On July 2, the 9th Pennsylvania Reserves received orders to hold the ground between the Round Tops. "Having gained the position designated, the line was fortified with the loose fragments of granite which lie scattered in profusion on the rugged sides of the mountain, and was made secure against attack."

Dedicated in 1890
39.789706, -77.23723; see map CC

815. 10th Pennsylvania Reserves (39th Pennsylvania Infantry)

The 10th Pennsylvania Reserves "swept along the rear and to the left of Little Round Top, driving the enemy back," and then occupied the low ground between the two hills. On the morning of July 3, the regiment moved forward and established defensive breastworks.

Dedicated in 1890
39.78868, –77.237636; see map CC

32. 11th Pennsylvania Infantry

The dog on the memorial to the 11th Pennsylvania is Sallie, the regiment's mascot. Although separated from the men when they retreated to Cemetery Hill, the brindle bull terrier remained where they had fought, with the dead and wounded, and rejoined the 11th Pennsylvania after the battle. She remained with them until struck and killed by a bullet at the Battle of Hatcher's Run in October 1864.

Dedicated in 1889
39.842139, –77.242614; see map B

723. 11th Pennsylvania Reserves (40th Pennsylvania Infantry)

Once the retreating regulars of the 5th Corps moved behind them on July 2, the soldiers of the Bloody Eleventh received the command to fire; "a terrible volley was delivered, which caused the foe to waver and turn." Then the reserves charged across the Valley of Death, with the 11th in the lead, "driving the enemy and deploying as it went."

Dedicated in 1890
39.796982, –77.240063; see map BB

836. 12th Pennsylvania Reserves (41st Pennsylvania)

After dark on July 2, the 12th Pennsylvania Reserves and the rest of its brigade received orders to take a position on top of Big Round Top. "Owing to the rugged nature of the ascent, and the darkness which prevailed, some confusion ensued," wrote historian Samuel Bates.

Dedicated in 1890
39.786212, -77.23927; see map FF

739. 13th Pennsylvania Reserves (The Bucktails)

The hunters and woodsmen of the 13th Pennsylvania Reserves wore deer tails in their caps and called themselves the Bucktails. On July 2, the regiment advanced on the left of their division, Col. Charles F. Taylor leading, toward a stone wall where "the impetuosity of the Bucktails was not to be denied, and in a few moments the Confederates were flying through the wheat field towards the woods at the farther side."

Dedicated in 1890
39.795177, -77.241286; see map BB

383. 16th Pennsylvania Cavalry

"Our regiment, part of it dismounted, held the ground near where the monument stands, on the 3rd of July, 1863," recalled a master sergeant of the 16th Pennsylvania Cavalry. The regiment provided "the connecting link between the cavalry and the infantry on that terrible field."

Dedicated in 1884
39.81761, -77.197696; see map Q

6. 17th Pennsylvania Cavalry

Under the command of Col. Josiah H. Kellogg, the 17th Pennsylvania Cavalry held its position here on July 1 until troops of the arriving 1st Corps relieved it.

Dedicated in 1889
39.84727, -77.245479; see map B

830. 18th Pennsylvania Cavalry Regiment

On July 3, division commander Judson Kilpatrick ordered the 1st Brigade's Elon Farnsworth to make a suicidal attack on the Confederates here. "All of a sudden the Rebs in our front appeared by the thousands," said Lt. Henry C. Potter of the 18th Pennsylvania Cavalry. "They seemed to come out of the ground like bees and they gave us such a rattling fire we all gave way and retreated."

Dedicated in 1889
39.784592, -77.24914; see map EE

634. 21st Pennsylvania Cavalry

Pvt. George W. Sandoe of the 21st Pennsylvania Cavalry, a local militia unit, became the first Union soldier to die at Gettysburg when he fell on June 26 in a clash with Confederate cavalry. There is a second monument to the regiment just to the south.

Dedicated in 1894
39.809129, -77.218617; see map Y

633. 21st Pennsylvania Cavalry

This is the second monument erected to the 21st Pennsylvania Cavalry. In this case private funding raised the money for the monument. The state-funded monument is just to the north.

39.808888, -77.218376; see map Y

847. 23rd Pennsylvania Infantry (Birney's Zouaves)

Originally commanded by David Birney, the 23rd Pennsylvania was also known as Birney's Zouaves. The regiment, with Lt. Col. John F. Glenn in command, received orders to support the 12th Corps on Culp's Hill. There, several companies "were met by so terrific a fire that they were compelled to lie down under protection of the line occupying the works."

Dedicated in 1886
39.817569, -77.219489; see map O

146. 26th Pennsylvania Emergency Militia

Raised hurriedly as Lee's army moved north, the 26th Pennsylvania Emergency Militia clashed with Jubal Early's troops on June 26 as the rebels passed through Gettysburg on their way to York. The green troops did not perform well against the seasoned Confederates.

Dedicated in 1892
39.830926, -77.236996; see map H

476. 26th Pennsylvania Infantry

The 26th Pennsylvania took up an exposed position on the right of the 3rd Corps, along the Emmitsburg Road, where it was "liable to be swept by artillery from the ridges beyond." While engaged with Florida troops, the regiment "charged the enemy and drove him in confusion across the road, making numerous captures," according to Bates's *History of Pennsylvania Volunteers*.

Dedicated in 1888
39.808936, -77.242969; see map V

148. 27th Pennsylvania Infantry

One of the regiments Gen. Oliver O. Howard held in reserve, the 27th Pennsylvania received orders on July 1 to advance and support the 11th Corps' retreat through Gettysburg. It fought a rearguard action at a brickyard here, a fight portrayed in the mural behind the monument. The regiment has a second monument on East Cemetery Hill.

Dedicated in 1884
39.835113, -77.228059; see map I

228. 27th Pennsylvania Infantry

Along with the 134th and 154th New York, the 27th Pennsylvania moved forward in a futile attempt to shore up the collapsing Union forces on July 1. (The regiment's first monument is on Coster Avenue.) After retreating to this spot on Cemetery Hill, the regiment participated in the defense against Jubal Early's division on the evening of July 2.

Dedicated in 1889
39.822022, -77.229753; see map N

331. 28th Pennsylvania Infantry

The 28th Pennsylvania was originally led by John Geary, who went on to command its division. At Gettysburg, wrote Samuel Bates in his *History of Pennsylvania Volunteers,* "the Twenty-eighth distinguished itself for its bravery and intrepidity."

Dedicated in 1885
39.818876, -77.219839; see map O

378. 28th Pennsylvania Infantry

The 28th Pennsylvania skirmished with the enemy from a position on the far right of the Union line until it was taken out and sent with the rest of John Geary's division to support the Union left. (Geary, the regiment's first colonel, took the wrong road and did not reach the fighting that day.)

Dedicated in 1905
39.81677, -77.214698; see map P

347. 29th Pennsylvania Infantry

This was the 29th Pennsylvania's original monument. During the fighting to regain their former breastworks, the regiment retired to replenish ammunition and then returned to the recaptured trenches, "where the men were much annoyed by sharpshooters." The regiment has a second monument, also on Culp's Hill.

Dedicated in 1885
39.816903, -77.220014; see map O

355. 29th Pennsylvania Infantry

Upon returning to Culp's Hill from the Union left late on July 2, the 29th Pennsylvania received fire from rebel soldiers who had occupied their works. Fighting began in earnest around 3:30 am. The rebels charged around 10:30. "It was a trying time for the Twenty-ninth, but the men stood manfully to their ground, firing with great rapidity, and doing fearful execution," wrote historian Samuel Bates. This is the regiment's second monument.

Dedicated in 1889
39.816434, -77.218326; see map O

364. 46th Pennsylvania Infantry

Returning from the Union left early on July 3 to discover Confederates holding their former breastworks, the Union soldiers of the 12th Corps prepared to retake them. The 46th Pennsylvania was on the right of the Union line and its loss, "owing to the sheltered position which the regiment occupied, was inconsiderable," wrote Samuel Bates in his five-volume history of Pennsylvania regiments.

Dedicated in 1889
39.815364, -77.217124; see map O

845. 49th Pennsylvania Infantry

On July 3, the 49th Pennsylvania received orders to support the 5th Corps, "but the enemy had now been repulsed and driven back at all points, and the battle was at an end. The regiment suffered no loss, though under a heavy artillery fire during the afternoon of the 3d."

Dedicated in 1889
39.7833, -77.227619; see map GG

713. 53rd Pennsylvania Infantry

As part of the brigade of Col. John R. Brooke (for whom Brooke Avenue is named), the 53rd Pennsylvania advanced against the rebels in the Wheatfield on July 2. The regiment had the brigade's right "in this terrible encounter, and suffered severely. It entered the engagement two hundred strong, and lost in killed and wounded upwards of eighty."

Dedicated in 1889
39.795484, -77.246495; see map BB

98. 56th Pennsylvania Infantry

The 56th Pennsylvania mustered in on October 16, 1861. At Gettysburg, its commander was Col. John W. Hofmann. On July 1, brigade commander Lysander Cutler told Hofmann the advancing soldiers were the enemy. "Turning to his men he commanded, 'Ready, right oblique, aim, fire!' and the Battle of Gettysburg was opened," remembered Cutler. "We suffered severely," wrote Hofmann. "In twenty minutes our loss in killed and wounded was over 70."

Dedicated in 1888
39.838947, -77.247318; see map G

498. 57th Pennsylvania Infantry

On July 2, the 57th Pennsylvania was "hotly engaged" when the enemy outflanked it on the left. Its right rested at the Sherfy house, and several men shooting from a cellar did not receive the order to retreat and were captured. The surviving members of the regiment moved to the rear and established a new line.

Dedicated in 1888
39.803719, -77.248626; see map V

646. 61ˢᵗ Pennsylvania Infantry

Reaching Gettysburg after an exhausting 36-mile forced march with the 6ᵗʰ Corps, the 61ˢᵗ Pennsylvania was ordered to this spot on the extreme right of the Union line. "Here four companies under Captain Creps, were on the picket line all day on the 3d, continually engaged with the enemy, the balance of the regiment being in the front line on the northerly slope of Wolf's Hill," read a regimental history.

Dedicated in 1888
39.80811, -77.208183; see map Z

705. 62ⁿᵈ Pennsylvania Infantry

Part of Col. Jacob Sweitzer's brigade of the 5ᵗʰ Corps' 1ˢᵗ Division, the 62ⁿᵈ Pennsylvania advanced into the Wheatfield on July 2. "The woods which surrounded the wheatfield seemed to be swarming with the enemy, every avenue of escape cut off, and the men terribly exposed in this open field," wrote historian Samuel Bates. The federals fought their way back toward Little Round Top, and the Pennsylvania Reserves charged forward in support.

Dedicated in 1889
39.795966, -77.244133; see map BB

461. 63ʳᵈ Pennsylvania Infantry

Raised by Alexander Hays (whose statue is near Ziegler's Grove), the 63ʳᵈ Pennsylvania moved forward as skirmishers on July 2. By 5:00 pm, its ammunition exhausted, the regiment withdrew, "having been nearly the entire day at the extreme front and uninterruptedly engaged since nine o'clock in the morning."

Dedicated in 1889
39.801786, -77.250128; see map U

470. 68ᵗʰ Pennsylvania Infantry (Scott Legion)

This is the original monument to the 68ᵗʰ Pennsylvania; the second is on the opposite side of the Peach Orchard, where it fought on July 2. "It was a terrible afternoon," said its colonel, Andrew H. Tippin, "and all were anxious for the Fifth Corps to come up, as we were being decimated by artillery."

Dedicated in 1886
39.800619, -77.250421; see map U

509. 68ᵗʰ Pennsylvania Infantry (Scott Legion)

On July 2, the 68ᵗʰ Pennsylvania held a position in the Peach Orchard. "As this was regarded as the key to the whole position, it was necessary to hold it at all hazards," wrote Samuel Bates. Around sunset the regiment, "greatly weakened by its losses and exhausted by frequent maneuverings," was forced to withdraw. The regiment's original monument is on the Emmitsburg Road.

Dedicated in 1888
39.801413, -77.249161; see map V

538. 69ᵗʰ Pennsylvania Infantry

Originally formed as the 3ʳᵈ California, the 69ᵗʰ Pennsylvania became part of the Keystone State's forces after the 1861 Battle of Ball's Bluff. As the harp on the shaft indicates, it was largely Irish. At Gettysburg, during the climax of Pickett's Charge, it was overwhelmed during brutal, close fighting that, one soldier said, "struck horror to us all."

Dedicated in 1887
39.812738, -77.236239; see map W

526. 71st Pennsylvania Infantry

The 71st Pennsylvania was originally called the 1st California Regiment because it was raised, mostly in Philadelphia, by Oregon senator Edward Baker to represent the Pacific coast. On July 3, the regiment's left wing was posted along the stone wall, with its right wing to the rear. Under the Confederate onslaught, the left wing fell back to the position held by the right.

39.813363, -77.236305; see map W

537. 72nd Pennsylvania Infantry (3rd California, Baxter's Fire Brigades, Philadelphia Fire Brigade)

As the Confederate attack crested on July 3, Gen. Alexander Webb ordered the 72nd Pennsylvania forward and even tried to grab the regimental flag from its bearer. The regiment did finally advance, but only after the Confederates were falling back. Survivors went to court to get their monument placed at this advanced point. A second monument marks their position 70 yards to the rear.

Dedicated in 1891
39.81295, -77.236318; see map W

529. 72nd Pennsylvania Infantry

This second monument marks the location, farther to the rear, occupied by the 72nd Pennsylvania on July 3, when Brig. Gen. Alexander Webb attempted to move them forward.

Dedicated in 1883
39.813019, -77.23568; see map W

229. 73rd Pennsylvania Infantry

The bronze bas-relief on the 73rd Pennsylvania's monument depicts the savage hand-to-hand struggle that took place here when the regiment fought against Harry Hays's Louisiana Tigers to save Wiedrich's Union battery. The regiment's commander was Capt. Daniel F. Kelley, who took over after Col. William Moore was wounded at Chancellorsville.

Dedicated in 1889
39.821921, -77.229224; see map N

47. 74th Pennsylvania Infantry

Col. Adolf von Hartung of the German 74th Pennsylvania took a bullet in the leg on July 1. Lt. Col. Alexander von Mitzel would not retreat until it was almost too late, and was captured. "To have been a member of the Seventy-fourth Pennsylvania is a prouder distinction than any patent of nobility that king or potentate might confer," said a veteran at the monument's dedication. A car knocked the monument over in 2003.

Dedicated in 1888
39.841207, -77.234219; see map C

58. 75th Pennsylvania Infantry

On July 1, the 75th Pennsylvania, a largely German regiment, engaged in severe, close-range fighting with Doles's brigade. One of the fatalities was Gettysburg native Lt. Henry Hauschild. Col. Francis Mahler, whose brother was killed, ordered a withdrawal before being mortally wounded himself. The regiment has a second monument in the National Cemetery.

Dedicated in 1888
39.84332, -77.229667; see map D

236. 75th Pennsylvania Infantry

During the fighting on July 1, the 75th Pennsylvania "engaged the enemy, and after a severe conflict, in which the regiment lost two officers and twenty-six men killed, six officers and ninety-four men wounded, and six prisoners, it fell back through the town with the remnants of the First Corps, and took position on Cemetery Hill."

Dedicated in 1886
39.821341, -77.230425; see map N

722. 81st Pennsylvania Infantry

Lt. Col. Amos Stroh led the 81st Pennsylvania after Col. H. Boyd McKeen took over brigade command. As one survivor recalled of the fighting on July 2, "[We] took our ground where ordered, stuck there, shot as fast as we could, and simply did our duty, then, as before and afterward."

Dedicated in 1889
39.796635, -77.241998; see map BB

337. 82nd Pennsylvania Infantry

Part of the 6th Corps, the 82nd Pennsylvania received orders on July 3 to support Geary's division of the 12th Corps on the Union right on Culp's Hill. "It was here exposed to a severe artillery fire," noted Samuel Bates in his *History of Pennsylvania Volunteers.* Once the situation stabilized here, the regiment returned to the Union left and then was posted in the center in reserve.

Dedicated in 1888
39.81776, -77.219643; see map O

811. 83rd Pennsylvania Infantry

Though officially an unidentified soldier, the likeness on top of the monument to the 83rd Pennsylvania is undoubtedly Col. Strong Vincent. He had been the regimental commander until promoted to brigade command. His regiments had barely arrived at Little Round Top when the rebels attacked, "with bayonets fixed and uttering unearthly yells." But the defenders prevailed.

Dedicated in 1889
39.790244, -77.237005; see map CC

583. 84th Pennsylvania Infantry

The 84th Pennsylvania guarded its division's supply wagons and forwarded supplies to the battlefield, "a vitally important duty, but one devoid of heroic incident," in the words of Samuel Bates in his history of Pennsylvania regiments. The diamonds in the monument's design refer to the 3rd Corps' diamond corps badge.

Dedicated in 1889
39.808216, -77.235278; see map W

24. 88th Pennsylvania Infantry

Fighting on July 1, the 88th Pennsylvania captured the flag of the 23rd Alabama, an action for which Sgt. Edward L. Gilligan later received the Medal of Honor. According to one survivor of the regiment at the monument's dedication in 1889, "[T]here was no heavier or harder fighting on any day, or on any part of the field, than right here on this line on the first day of the battle."

Dedicated in 1889
39.843386, -77.242083; see map B

23. 88th Pennsylvania Infantry

This marker indicates where the 88th Pennsylvania charged forward on July 1, capturing "many prisoners and the flags of the 23rd North Carolina and the 26th Alabama." The regiment's primary monument is on Doubleday Avenue.

39.843609, -77.242884; see map B

280. 88th Pennsylvania Infantry (Cameron Light Guard)

The 88th Pennsylvania was first called the Cameron Light Guard after then-secretary of war Simon Cameron. On July 2, the 88th was posted here and sent forward as reinforcements to help repulse Pickett's Charge. The regiment's main monument is on Doubleday Avenue, where the 88th fought on July 1.

39.817081, -77.233985; see map N

604. 88th Pennsylvania

One of this regiment's four markers, this small one indicates its position on July 2, when it fought to stop the Confederate assault. The 88th "did its full share in the repulse," notes the history *Pennsylvania at Gettysburg.*

39.806505, -77.234951; see map W

21. 90th Pennsylvania Infantry

Maj. Alfred J. Sellers of the 90th Pennsylvania earned the Medal of Honor for his actions on July 1, when he succeeded in having the regiment change front and resist the enemy attack from the north. The regiment has one of the more unusual monuments on the battlefield. The story goes that after a cannonball hit an oak, one of the regiment's soldiers carefully recovered a bird's nest and replaced it in the shattered trunk.

Dedicated in 1888
39.844363, -77.24205; see map B

605. 90th Pennsylvania Infantry

This is one of three monuments to the 90th Pennsylvania and indicates its position on July 2, when, "after taking up a position with our depleted numbers on Cemetery Hill, we supported batteries," as an officer recalled at the dedication of the regiment's main monument, on Doubleday Avenue.

Dedicated in 1889
39.806369, -77.234917; see map W

282. 90th Pennsylvania Infantry

The 90th Pennsylvania has three monuments on the battlefield. This one commemorates its July 3 actions. On the battle's 25th anniversary, Alfred Sellers, who took charge when Col. Peter Lyle assumed brigade command, told his veterans, "[Y]ou were brought over on the double-quick to support the Second Corps, and arrived just in time to witness the collapse, men of the vanquished Confederates passing through our line to the rear."

Dedicated in 1888
39.816846, -77.234573; see map N

802. 91st Pennsylvania Infantry

On July 2, the 91st Pennsylvania received orders to move at double-quick to defend Little Round Top. "Our brigade marched up one side of Little Round Top, as the rebels charged up the other, and was thrown into line to meet them," said the brigade commander.

Dedicated in 1889
39.792125, -77.236776; see map CC

786. 93rd Pennsylvania Infantry

The 93rd Pennsylvania has two monuments on the battlefield. The 6th Corps' Gen. John Sedgwick personally positioned the unit on this spot. The second monument marks where it advanced into the Wheatfield.

Dedicated in 1884
39.796077, -77.234695; see map CC

769. 93rd Pennsylvania Infantry

The 93rd Pennsylvania reached the field on July 2, as the 3rd Corps was being forced back. Ordered to conceal itself until the enemy came close, "impatience got better of obedience and discretion" and the regiment opened fire early; "after a short contest the rebel line was driven in tumult."

Dedicated 1888
39.796925, -77.237543; see map CC

774. 95th Pennsylvania Infantry (Gosline Zouaves)

Also known as the Gosline Zouaves, after Col. John M. Gosline, the 95th Pennsylvania Infantry reached this spot at the end of the 6th Corps' forced march on July 2. It suffered one killed and six wounded.

Dedicated in 1888
39.795396, -77.236494; see map CC

773. 96th Pennsylvania Infantry

The 96th Pennsylvania Infantry originated from the National Light Infantry of Pottsville, one of the "First Defenders" who reached Washington when war broke out. "Foot sore and weary," the regiment reached the Gettysburg Battlefield on July 2 and "took position behind a stone fence which it held with slight loss until the close of the battle."

Dedicated in 1888
39.796117, -77.237724; see map CC

795. 98th Pennsylvania Infantry

Upon reaching the battlefield after the 6th Corps' forced march on July 2, the 98th Pennsylvania took a position on the right of its brigade on this shoulder of Little Round Top. As the 3rd Corps was driven back, the brigade "held its position unmoved, and on the following day advanced a little." Most of its casualties came from sharpshooters. The regiment has another monument near the Weikert farmhouse.

Dedicated in 1884
39.793719, -77.235913; see map CC

766. 98th Pennsylvania Infantry

After an epic forced march with the 6th Corps, the 98th Pennsylvania reached the field on July 2 and took position here. The brigade remained in place as the 3rd Corps was forced back. "During the whole of the 3d, the regiment was lying in the front line of battle, exposed to the enemy's fire, but protected by a stone wall," reported Maj. John B. Kohler.

Dedicated in 1889
39.797609, -77.236622; see map CC

754. 99th Pennsylvania Infantry

On July 2, the 99th Pennsylvania formed the left of its brigade in Sickles's advanced position at Devil's Den. It had barely formed its line "when the storm of battle burst upon it, and raged with a fury scarcely paralleled." With only an 18-inch wall as breastworks, the 99th held its ground until relieved, "leaving half its number killed or wounded on the field." The regiment's original monument now stands on Hancock Avenue.

Dedicated in 1889
39.792376, -77.242257; see map BB

524. 99th Pennsylvania Infantry

This monument stood at Devil's Den until it was replaced in 1889 by the one that stands there now. Maj. John W. Moore was wounded while in command of the regiment on July 2 but managed to resume command on July 3. The regiment helped Battery A, 4th U.S. Artillery, withdraw its guns so they wouldn't be captured.

Dedicated in 1886; moved in 1889
39.813502, -77.235172; see map W

767. 102nd Pennsylvania Infantry

The 102nd Pennsylvania reached the field at Gettysburg on July 2 "after a long and wearisome march." It took this position near Little Round Top until it "was withdrawn a short distance," where it remained "with only slight loss, until the close of the struggle."

Dedicated in 1889
39.79752, -77.237022; see map C

496. 105th Pennsylvania Infantry (The Wild Cat Regiment)

Formed in a Congressional district called the Wild Cat District, the 105th Pennsylvania fought here on July 2 against increasing pressure from enemy infantry. "Finally the line on its left was broken through, and the rebels came pouring in upon its flank and rear, compelling it to fall back." According to its colonel, Calvin Craig, "the boys fought like demons."

Dedicated in 1889
39.804305, -77.247891; see map V

473. 106th Pennsylvania Infantry

On July 2, the 106th Pennsylvania advanced to attack Wright's brigade of Georgians. "Promptly and well was the movement executed," remembered an officer. The regiment took prisoners and recaptured three Union guns before being sent to assist the 11th Corps on Cemetery Hill.

Dedicated in 1885
39.811594, -77.239979; see map V

540. 106ᵗʰ Pennsylvania Infantry

One of three monuments or markers to the 106ᵗʰ Pennsylvania, this one indicates the site where two of the regiment's companies engaged in brutal fighting around the Copse of Trees on July 3, as the Confederacy reached its "high-water mark." The bas-relief depicts the regiment advancing toward the Codori house near the Emmitsburg Road on July 2.

Dedicated in 1886
39.812639, -77.235553; see map W

224. 106ᵗʰ Pennsylvania Infantry

This marker indicates the 106ᵗʰ Pennsylvania's position on July 3. "You can be withdrawn when that regiment runs away," Gen. Howard told his artillery chief on July 1, indicating the 106ᵗʰ. The regiment also has monuments on the Emmitsburg Road and near the Copse of Trees on Hancock Avenue.

39.822317, -77.229465; see map N

33. 107ᵗʰ Pennsylvania Infantry

The 107ᵗʰ Pennsylvania advanced to a stone wall near here on July 1, "the men loading as they walked," wrote Lt. Col. James Mac-Thomson in his official report. "Here it was where our regiment made the fight, and a good one it was," recalled an officer.

Dedicated in 1889
39.841902, -77.242666; see map B

203. 107th Pennsylvania Infantry

This marker indicates where the 107th Pennsylvania was on July 2; its main monument is on Doubleday Avenue. "Our casualties during the second day were 1 commisioned officer and several men wounded," reported Capt. Emanuel D. Roath.

39.815533, -77.235259; see map M

349. 109th Pennsylvania Infantry

The 109th Pennsylvania returned to Culp's Hill late on July 2 to hear a challenge from their former breastworks. Upon identifying themselves, "a terrible fire of musketry was opened upon the command." In the morning the regiment helped drive away the rebels who had been occupying the position. "Our loss was small, owing to our strong defensive position," reported Capt. Frederick Gimber.

Dedicated in 1889
39.816944, -77.219412; see map O

711. 110th Pennsylvania Infantry

Under the command of Lt. Col. David M. Jones, the 110th Pennsylvania advanced almost to the Emmitsburg Road on July 2, where it faced the attacking Confederates in the afternoon. "With desperation, the rebel horde came on, but was again and again swept back by the steady fire of the One Hundred and Tenth and the Fifth Michigan," until the federals withdrew. Wounded, Jones lost a leg.

Dedicated in 1889
39.796557, -77.246124; see map BB

353. 111th Pennsylvania Infantry

The 111th Pennsylvania returned to Culp's Hill late on July 2 to find their breastworks occupied by the enemy. The Union troops drove the rebels out in a fierce battle the next morning. After the fighting, Col. George Cobham Jr. wrote to his brother that the ground all around him was covered with the dead, "and the blood is standing in pools all around me; it is a sickening sight."

Dedicated in 1889
39.816733, -77.218773; see map O

499. 114th Pennsylvania Infantry (Collis's Zouaves)

Named after their colonel, Charles Collis (who had been wounded at Chancellorsville), the 114th Pennsylvania was a brightly garbed Zouave regiment. On July 2, rebel infantry outflanked the regiment and "compelled it to retire." Among the captured was its commander, Lt. Col. Frederick F. Cavada.

Dedicated in 1886
39.803525, -77.248658; see map V

525. 114th Pennsylvania Infantry (Collis's Zouaves)

Also known as Collis's Zouaves, the 114th Pennsylvania has a second, more elaborate, monument near the Sherfy farmhouse on the Emmitsburg Road. Its commander, Frederick Cavada, was captured on July 2, and Capt. Edward R. Bowen took over. There's a monument to the regiment's original commander, Charles Collis, in the National Cemetery.

Dedicated in 1902
39.813497, -77.23464; see map W

707. 115th Pennsylvania

Outflanked in the Wheatfield on July 2, the 115th Pennsylvania withdrew, stopping to support a beleaguered Union battery. "Halting and quickly reforming, it checked the mad onset of the enemy until the guns could be limbered and taken away, when it was ordered to kneel in the tall grass again and open fire."

Dedicated in 1889
39.795701, -77.244724; see map BB

686. 116th Pennsylvania Infantry

Part of the Irish Brigade and commanded by Maj. St. Clair A. Mulholland, the 116th Pennsylvania moved into the Wheatfield on July 2. "The struggle was desperate." Despite initial triumph, the federals found themselves being outflanked and had to "retire rapidly, but in tolerable good order."

Dedicated in 1888
39.797525, -77.245961; see map BB

683. 118th Pennsylvania Infantry
(The Corn Exchange Regiment)

The 118th Pennsylvania was held in reserve until the afternoon of July 2, when it went forward to support the retreating 3rd Corps. There the regiment became "hotly engaged." That night the regiment "slept on their arms in line during the night, the enemy being completely checked," wrote historian Samuel Bates.

Dedicated in 1889
39.797664, -77.246934; see map BB

679. 118th Pennsylvania Infantry (The Corn Exchange Regiment)

This marker on Wheatfield Road indicates the second position of the 118th Pennsylvania (the Corn Exchange Regiment) on July 2.

39.799144, -77.243722; see map BB

763. 118th Pennsylvania Infantry (The Corn Exchange Regiment)

The 118th Pennsylvania has two monuments and a marker on the battlefield. After fighting in the Wheatfield on July 2, it moved to Big Round Top, "where it remained behind breast-works, undisturbed, except by the enemy's sharp-shooters, until the close of the battle."

Dedicated in 1884–1885
39.78749, -77.238372; see map BB

841. 119th Pennsylvania Infantry

The 119th Pennsylvania reached the battlefield with the 6th Corps on July 2, and the next morning moved to this position, "but did not become engaged, the enemy making no determined demonstration on that part of the field." The regiment has another monument on Big Round Top.

Dedicated in 1888
39.783832, -77.229369; see map GG

833. 119ᵗʰ Pennsylvania Infantry

The 119ᵗʰ Pennsylvania made the exhausting 36-mile march with the 6ᵗʰ Corps, arriving on the afternoon of July 2. The next morning, it moved to the far left of the Union line, and it took up its position here on the evening of July 3. It has another monument on Howe Avenue.

Dedicated in 1885
39.786723, -77.23934; see map FF

124. 121ˢᵗ Pennsylvania Infantry

The 121ˢᵗ Pennsylvania formed the extreme left of the Union position when it reached the field on July 1 and faced the advancing men of Heth's division. Finally outflanked, the regiment fell back to Seminary Ridge and then through Gettysburg to Cemetery Hill. "At no time was there any panic," wrote its commanding officer, Maj. Alexander Biddle. (His cousin, Chapman Biddle, commanded the brigade.) There's another monument to the 121ˢᵗ on Hancock Avenue.

Dedicated in 1889
39.830548, -77.251628; see map G

554. 121ˢᵗ Pennsylvania Infantry

This is one of two monuments to the 121ˢᵗ Pennsylvania (the other is on Reynolds Avenue and commemorates its action on July 1). On July 3, the regiment was here, prepared to support the defense of Cemetery Ridge.

Dedicated in 1886
39.810966, -77.23547; see map W

506. 139th Pennsylvania Infantry

The 139th Pennsylvania arrived on the field with the 6th Corps on the afternoon of July 2. "Here it took up a position which it held, checking the enemy in every attempt to penetrate the Union lines." The regiment has a second monument by the Weikert farm.

Dedicated in 1886
39.801075, -77.247056; see map V

772. 139th Pennsylvania Infantry

After completing the 6th Corps' forced march to Gettysburg, the 139th Pennsylvania and its brigade took up its position here on July 2. When soldiers of the V Corps fell back, "we delivered two volleys, and then charged on the enemy, driving him back in disorder," reported Lieutenant Colonel William H. Moody.

Dedicated in 1889
39.79658, -77.237869; see map CC

687. 140th Pennsylvania Infantry

This is the original monument to the 140th Pennsylvania, which fought in the Wheatfield on July 2 as part of Caldwell's brigade of the 2nd Corps. After withstanding withering fire from the advancing Confederates, the Pennsylvanians withdrew.

Dedicated in 1885
39.797613, -77.245595; see map BB

684. 140th Pennsylvania Infantry

Part of Caldwell's division of the 2nd Corps, sent to aid the overextended 3rd on July 2, the 140th Pennsylvania pushed forward into the Wheatfield "in the face of a severe fire" and reached the ridge here. "But this advantage, gained at fearful cost, was of no avail," reads Bates's *History of Pennsylvania Volunteers*; the federals had to withdraw. The regiment's original monument is nearby.

Dedicated in 1889
39.79764, -77.24618; see map BB

510. 141st Pennsylvania Infantry

Positioned at the salient in Sickles's line at the Peach Orchard, the 141st Pennsylvania supported the batteries here until forced to withdraw. "Though fearfully torn, the regiment preserved a bold front, and again and again rallied and turned upon the foe," until it formed a new line, supported by soldiers of the 5th Corps. Its losses were around 70 percent—among the Union regiments who fought at Gettysburg, only the 1st Minnesota suffered more.

Dedicated in 1889
39.80108, -77.248776; see map V

119. 142nd Pennsylvania Infantry

The 142nd Pennsylvania arrived on the field with the 1st Corps on July 1 and was eventually outflanked by the advancing Confederate troops and forced to fall back to Seminary Ridge and then to Cemetery Hill. Its colonel, Robert P. Cummins, was mortally wounded here. He died the next day.

Dedicated in 1889
39.83275, -77.25088; see map G

109. 143rd Pennsylvania Infantry

Captured in stone, Sgt. Ben Crippen, the 143rd Pennsylvania's color bearer, permanently shakes his fist in the direction from which the Confederates advanced. Part of Doubleday's division of the 1st Corps, the 143rd was falling back from the rebels on July 1 when Crippen expressed his defiance. He paid the ultimate price, falling to enemy bullets. The regiment saved its colors and retreated through Gettysburg and up Cemetery Hill.

Dedicated in 1895
39.836641, -77.249306; see map G

566. 143rd Pennsylvania Infantry

The 143rd Pennsylvania's main monument is on the Chambersburg Pike, where it fought on July 1. This marker indicates the position the regiment held on July 2 and 3. "I have the honor to report that all my command stood at their posts amid all the iron that filled the air," noted Lt. Col. John D. Musser.

39.809811, -77.236181; see map W

712. 145th Pennsylvania Infantry

The 145th Pennsylvania, part of the 2nd Corps' 1st Division, went to support the 3rd Corps on July 2. Initially, they pushed the men of Kershaw's brigade from the Wheatfield, where the Confederates "halted and sent a deadly fire of lead into the Union ranks." The tide turned as the Confederates threatened to outflank the federals, and the 145th fell back.

Dedicated in 1889
39.795704, -77.24704; see map BB

366. 147th Pennsylvania Infantry

The star indicates that the 147th Pennsylvania belonged to the 12th Corps, which used the star as its corps insignia. The regiment returned from the Union left late on July 2 to find rebels in their breastworks. They began fighting the enemy before dawn on July 3, and "until ten o'clock am, the firing was incessant, fresh ammunition being brought up and distributed to the men as the supply became exhausted."

Dedicated in 1882
39.815771, -77.220421; see map O

367. 147th Pennsylvania Infantry

This monument to the 147th Pennsylvania is in Pardee Field, a clearing named after the regiment's commander, Lt. Col. Ario Pardee Jr. The fighting here was bloody, but the 147th had light casualties "in comparison with that which it inflicted, and with the vital nature of the struggle," wrote Samuel Bates in his *History of Pennsylvania Volunteers*.

Dedicated in 1905
39.815676, -77.219623; see map O

792. 147th Pennsylvania Infantry

Moved over from Culp's Hill late on July 2, the 147th Pennsylvania arrived to find that the fighting here had ended. It returned to Culp's Hill, where the regiment has two monuments.

39.794496, -77.234454; see map CC

728. 148th Pennsylvania Infantry

On July 2, the 148th Pennsylvania advanced into the Wheatfield. "The men displayed admirable coolness, and in general took deliberate aim before firing," said a regimental history. After an hour of fighting, "the line was relieved, and fell back in good order, occupying the position held in the morning." The regiment has a second monument on Hancock Avenue.

Dedicated in 1901
39.795985, -77.242; see map BB

608. 148th Pennsylvania Infantry

This marker indicates the 148th Pennsylvania's position on July 3, when the enemy "was triumphantly repulsed by troops to our right," according to a regimental record. Its principal monument is in the Wheatfield, where the regiment fought on July 2.

Dedicated in 1901
39.805408, -77.234819; see map W

84. 149th Pennsylvania (1st Regiment, Bucktail Brigade)

The 149th Pennsylvania was not the original "Bucktails." The 13th Pennsylvania Reserves were, and some of its members did not take kindly to the "bogus" Bucktails taking their name. Nonetheless, the 149th Pennsylvania fought valiantly on July 1, with color sergeant Henry Brehm being cut down near the McPherson barn as he tried to save the regimental colors.

Dedicated 1888
39.837612, -77.251429; see map G

564. 149th Pennsylvania Infantry (1st Regiment, Bucktail Brigade)

On July 3, the regiment remained here in support of Stannard's Vermont brigade when the Vermonters attacked the advancing Confederates' flank. This was the regiment's first monument, moved here after being replaced by the one that now stands on Chambersburg Pike. There's also a monument to Company D on West Confederate Avenue.

Dedicated in 1886
39.810125, -77.235811; see map W

134. 149th Pennsylvania Infantry, Company D

As the Union forces fell back on July 1, Company D of the 149th Pennsylvania fought a rearguard action here, opening "a fire sufficient to induce the enemy to halt, supposing that our forces had made a stand there." The 20-minute delay provided time for Union artillery to remove all their guns but one.

39.829666, -77.244163; see map H

87. 150th Pennsylvania (2nd Regiment, Bucktail Brigade)

The 150th Pennsylvania, the second regiment of the Bucktail Brigade, distinguished itself with hard fighting around the McPherson barn on July 1. Its commander, Col. Langhorne Wister, took command of the brigade and was wounded in the face. The 150th then retreated through the town, where its flag was captured, and up Cemetery Hill.

Dedicated in 1889
39.83684, -77.252247; see map G

560. 150ᵗʰ Pennsylvania Infantry (2ⁿᵈ Regiment, Bucktail Brigade)

The 150ᵗʰ Pennsylvania saw hard fighting on July 1 and has another monument on Reynolds Avenue. On July 2, the regiment advanced to the Emmitsburg Road and served as skirmishers; from the site of this monument, it helped repulse the Confederate attack on July 3.

Dedicated in 1888
39.81061, -77.235477; see map W

116. 151ˢᵗ Pennsylvania

Col. George McFarland counted 113 schoolteachers on the 151ˢᵗ Pennsylvania's rolls when the regiment formed in October 1862. On July 1, the 151ˢᵗ suffered from "galling fire" on both its flanks until McFarland ordered it back to Seminary Ridge, where he was badly wounded in the legs (his right leg was amputated). "I know not how men could have fought more desperately, exhibited more coolness, or contested the field with more determined courage than did those of the One hundred and fifty-first Pennsylvania Volunteers on that ever-memorable day," recalled McFarland.

Dedicated in 1888
39.833755, -77.250995; see map G

CIVILIANS AT GETTYSBURG

Despite the fighting that raged through Gettysburg on July 1 and the subsequent shelling and shooting that took place in and around the town for the rest of the conflict, only one civilian died during the battle. Mary Virginia "Jennie" Wade was making bread at her sister's house on July 3 when a bullet passed through two doors and hit her in the back. The building is a museum today. Two citizens, John Burns and Elizabeth Thorn, have battlefield statues today; the Burns statute is on Stone Avenue and Thorn's is in Evergreen Cemetery, where she, Burns, and Wade are all buried.

68. 153rd Pennsylvania Infantry

A largely German regiment, the 153rd Pennsylvania had mustered in for nine months and its enlistments were due to end in just a few weeks. "This beautiful monument . . . will, as the years roll on, tell the story of what you did here, and it will serve to keep green the memories of those of our comrades that fell here," Lt. William Beidelman told surviving veterans in 1889.

Dedicated in 1889
39.845672, -77.226151; see map D

246. 153rd Pennsylvania Infantry

The 153rd Pennsylvania fought here on the evening of July 2 against Avery's North Carolinians, using "clubs, knives, stones, fists—anything calculated to inflict death or pain was resorted to." In the 1990s, vandals knocked this monument over to steal a time capsule from its base. The regiment has its main monument on Howard Avenue.

Dedicated in 1884
39.821547, -77.227336; see map N

798. 155th Pennsylvania Infantry

The 155th Pennsylvania reached the battlefield with the rest of the 5th Corps on July 2 and received orders to hold Little Round Top with the rest of the brigade. The regiment gained "the very crest of the Mount," said Bates's history of Pennsylvania regiments. On July 3, the 155th was able to watch the Confederate attack of Pickett's Charge from this vantage point.

Dedicated in 1886
39.793008, -77.236431; see map CC

581. C&F Independent Pennsylvania Artillery (Thompson's and Hampton's Batteries)

Also known as Thompson's and Hampton's Batteries, the units of this consolidated unit also have separate monuments in the Peach Orchard, where they fought on the afternoon of July 2.

Dedicated in 1885
39.807376, -77.235596; see map W

324. Pennsylvania Independent Battery E (Knap's Battery)

Formed from men of the 28th Pennsylvania under Capt. Joseph M. Knap (who left in May 1863 to take charge of the Fort Pitt Foundry in Pittsburgh), Pennsylvania Independent Battery E had six guns. One of its officers was Lt. Edward Geary, the general's son, who would die in the fighting at Chattanooga in October 1863. The battery has another monument on Power's Hill.

Dedicated in 1889
39.819941, -77.220147; see map O

468. Pennsylvania Light Artillery, Battery C (Thompson's Battery)

Recruited in Pittsburgh by Capt. James Thompson, Battery C was consolidated with Hampton's Battery F in June, and they fought together at Gettysburg, with Thompson in overall command. The batteries, at an angle in Sickles's line, had two guns facing west and four south. It lost one gun during the withdrawal. There's a monument to the consolidated batteries on Hancock Avenue.

Dedicated in 1886
39.801407, -77.249692; see map U

638. Pennsylvania Light Artillery, Battery E (Knap's Battery)

Two guns of this battery were posted on the 12th Corps' far right, under Lt. Edward Geary, Gen. John Geary's son. Four more guns stayed with the 2nd Corps on July 1 but rejoined the 12th Corps after that.

Dedicated in 1897
39.806428, -77.219717; see map Y

508. Pennsylvania Light Artillery, Battery F (Hampton's Battery)

Raised in Pittsburgh by Capt. Robert B. Hampton, who was killed at Chancellorsville, Hampton's Battery was consolidated with Thompson's Battery on June 3. It held its position in the Peach Orchard until the 3rd Corps' collapse compelled it to withdraw.

Dedicated in 1886
39.801404, -77.249436; see map V

586. Pennsylvania State Monument

The battlefield's largest memorial, the 110-foot-tall Pennsylvania State Monument weighs 3,840 tons and is crowned by the Goddess of Victory and Peace. Statues of Pennsylvania generals line the perimeter. They include George Meade, John Reynolds, Alfred Pleasonton, David McMurtrie Gregg, and Winfield Scott Hancock, plus wartime governor Andrew Gregg Curtin and president Abraham Lincoln. Ninety bronze tablets list the names of all 34,530 soldiers from Pennsylvania who served during the Civil War.

Dedicated on September 27, 1910
39.807585, -77.235063; see map W

RHODE ISLAND

521. 1st Rhode Island Artillery, Battery A (Arnold's Battery)

Known as Arnold's Battery after its commander, Capt. William Arnold, the battery suffered so badly during the Confederate bombardment on July 3 that its crews had to limber up and move back.

Dedicated in 1886
39.813575, -77.235528; see map W

849. 1st Rhode Island Light Artillery, Battery B (Brown's Battery)

On July 2, Battery B of the 1st Rhode Island Artillery "was exposed to a most severe infantry fire; 24 horses were killed and 6 disabled, and it became necessary to send two guns to the rear." This small marker indicates the battery's position. As the enemy rapidly advanced, "we succeeded in retiring with four pieces leaving two on the field, the horses having been killed."

39.812201,-77.237561; see map W

543. 1st Rhode Island Artillery, Battery B (Brown's Battery)

This monument marks the position of Battery B, 1st Rhode Island Artillery, on July 3, when it suffered from the artillery barrage before Pickett's Charge. "It was terrible beyond description; the air was full of shell hissing and bursting," wrote one sergeant. Relieved by the 1st New York Independent Battery, Brown's men moved to the rear.

39.812312, -77.23543; see map W

460. 1st Rhode Island Artillery, Battery E (Randolph's Battery)

Also known as Randolph's battery after its former commander, Battery E of the 1st Rhode Island Artillery was led by Lt. John K. Bucklyn. The battery withstood heavy fire on July 2. "Lieutenant Bucklyn, always brave and daring, now that death and destruction appeared almost inevitable, seemed, if possible, to show more daring as the danger increased." He was wounded, one of 29 casualties.

Dedicated in 1886
39.802329, -77.24941; see map U

790. 2nd Rhode Island Infantry

Acting as a reserve and positioned here on July 2, the 2nd Rhode Island suffered light casualties, with one man dying. Elisha Hunt Rhodes, whose letters played a major role in Ken Burns's Civil War series, served in the regiment's Company B.

Dedicated in 1886
39.795734, -77.234215; see map CC

475. 2nd Rhode Island Infantry

This small marker indicates the position of the 2nd Rhode Island's skirmish line on July 4. Its primary monument is on Sedgwick Avenue.

39.809822, -77.242196; see map V

SOUTH CAROLINA

658. South Carolina State Monument

South Carolina was the first state to secede from the Union (on December 20, 1861) and the state where the Civil War started, when secessionists fired on Fort Sumter in Charleston Harbor. The South Carolina monument is one of several to Southern states erected during the war's centennial. It stands near the spot where Kershaw's South Carolinian brigade formed for the attack on July 2.

Dedicated in 1963
39.797762, -77.25589; see map AA

TENNESSEE

193. Tennessee State Monument

Tennessee was a divided state during the war, with Union sentiment strongest in the east. In January 1861, voters were four to one against secession, but governor Isham Harris established connections with the Confederacy anyway. Abraham Lincoln later appointed Andrew Johnson of Tennessee as military governor. Three Tennessee regiments, the 1st, 7th, and 14th, fought at Gettysburg.

Dedicated in 1982
39.817702, -77.247914; see map L

THE GETTYSBURG BATTLEFIELD MEMORIAL ASSOCIATION

Pennsylvania's legislature approved the incorporation of the Gettysburg Battlefield Monument Association in 1864. The association's object was to "hold, and preserve, the battle-grounds of Gettysburg." The GBMA encouraged states and veteran groups to raise money for monuments and oversaw the positions where they were placed. The GBMA also decreed that monuments be made from granite instead of softer limestone, sandstone, or marble (with a few exceptions). This is one reason why Gettysburg's monuments remain in good shape today.

TEXAS

672. The Texas Brigade

Often called Hood's Texas Brigade after former commander John Bell Hood (who was leading the division at Gettysburg), this unit had a well-deserved reputation as tenacious fighters. At Gettysburg, its four regiments (three from Texas and one from Arkansas), under the command of Brig. Gen. Jerome Robertson, moved out from here to attack the Union left on July 2. Robertson, who was wounded, called it "the hardest fought battle of the war in which I have been engaged."

Dedicated in 1913
39.790261, -77.254407; see map AA

674. Texas State Monument

Texas citizens voted to secede from the Union on February 23, 1861, and on March 5, the secession convention voted to join the Confederacy. Up to 60,000 Texans served in the rebel armies. The most famous Lone Star unit at Gettysburg was Hood's Texas Brigade, under the command of Maj. Gen. Jerome B. Robertson (like Hood, a native of Kentucky). The state's monument, dedicated in 1964, is identical to those placed on ten other Civil War battlefields.

Dedicated in 1864
39.790116, -77.25432; see map AA

SOUTHERN MONUMENTS AT GETTYSBURG

Union monuments greatly outnumber the Confederate ones at Gettysburg. As the site of a Union victory, in a Northern state, Gettysburg held less appeal to Confederate veterans than to their Union counterparts. The GBMA also resisted the idea of commemorating Southern feats of arms. The first Confederate monument, to the 1st Maryland Infantry (which the GBMA called the 2nd Maryland to avoid confusion with a Union regiment of the same name), went up in 1886. Others were slow to follow.

VERMONT

838. 1st Vermont Brigade

The 1st Vermont Brigade consisted of five regiments from the state—the 2nd through the 6th. Arriving with the 6th Corps after its forced march, the Vermonters went to the army's left, where "they saw but little of the fighting which shook the solid ground beneath their feet, and suffered no loss."

Dedicated in 1889
39.78506, -77.232285; see map GG

762. 1st Vermont Cavalry

Part of Elon Farnsworth's brigade, the 1st Vermont took part in the doomed attack ordered by Judson Kilpatrick on July 3 and soon encountered deadly Confederate fire. "Every time a man near was hit I could hear the pat of the bullet," recalled the regiment's bugler.

Dedicated in 1889
39.786923, -77.24369; see map BB

568. 13th Vermont Infantry

Col. Francis V. Randall was leading the 13th Vermont into battle on July 2 when his horse was killed and fell on top of him. He caught up as the regiment participated in a devastating flank attack on the 22nd Georgia. The statue on the monument is of Lt. Stephen F. Brown, who carried a hatchet into battle because he had been relieved of his sword after allowing his men to fetch water despite orders.

Dedicated in 1899
39.809684, -77.236286; see map W

569. 13th Vermont Infantry

The 13th Vermont is represented four times on the battlefield. Its main monument is on Hancock Avenue and the other three mark various positions it held on July 3. This marker shows the 13th Vermont's first position on that day, where it and the rest of Brig. Gen. George J. Stannard's 2nd Vermont Brigade withstood the Confederate bombardment prior to Pickett's Charge.

39.809616, -77.236142; see map W

567. 13th Vermont Infantry

This small marker indicates the 13th Vermont's second position on July 3. As the Confederates advanced, the rebels on the right columns shifted to the north. Brig. Gen. Stannard ordered his men to make a flank attack, acting "with a decision and promptitude which did him infinite credit," noted *Vermont in the Civil War*.

39.809716, -77.236705; see map W

549. 13th Vermont Infantry

This marker indicates the third position of the 13th Vermont on July 3, when the regiment fired into the advancing rebel flank from close range. "The effect unpon the Confederate mass was instantaneous. Its progress ceased . . . . Their dead and wounded and small arms by thousands strewed the ground over which they charged," recounted *Vermont in the Civil War*.

39.811503, -77.236647; see map W

574. 14th Vermont Infantry

Commanded by William T. Nichols, a former lawyer from Rutland, the 14th Vermont helped repulse Confederate brigades sent to reinforce the men of Pickett's Charge near the climax of the fighting on July 3.

Dedicated in 1899
39.808901, -77.236606; see map W

572. 16th Vermont Infantry

Along with the 13th Vermont, the 16th Vermont of Stannard's brigade attacked the rebels' right flank on July 3. "With a mighty shout the rush forward was made, and, before the enemy could change his front we had struck his flank and swept down the line," said its colonel, Wheelock G. Veazy, who won the Medal of Honor for his actions that day.

Dedicated in 1892
39.809249, -77.236549; see map W

760. Vermont Sharpshooters (Companies E & H, 2nd Regiment United States Sharpshooters)

On July 2, the Vermont sharpshooters met the advancing Confederates of Law's brigade. "The sharpshooters held their position till Law's line was within 100 yards, when the order to fall back firing was given and the sharpshooters retired, a few of the bulldogs of the regiment lingering to fire one more shot, till they were fairly crowded in before the advancing bayonets."

Dedicated in 1889
39.788931, -77.246884; see map BB

> *"The Vermonters were eminently men of peace; but they won honorable distinction as soldiers. The history of the war cannot be written without frequent and honorable mention of them."*
>
> —George Grenville Benedict in *Vermont in the Civil War*

437. Vermont Sharpshooters (Company F, 1st U.S. Sharpshooters)

Organized by the sometimes controversial Hiram Berdan, the United States Sharpshooters wore unique green uniforms and carried breech-loading Sharps rifles. On July 2, this company of Vermont sharpshooters advanced with four other companies into Pitzer Woods, where they stumbled into Wilcox's Alabamians. "Berdan was attacked sharply in return, and forced to retire with a severe loss," said *New York at Gettysburg*.

Dedicated in 1889
39.808093, -77.257334; see map U

570. Vermont State Monument

A statue of Brig. Gen. George Stannard stands at the top of the Vermont State Monument. The first soldier from Vermont to volunteer for the war, Stannard had been captured at Harpers Ferry in September 1862 and paroled. He took command of the 2nd Vermont Brigade in April 1863 and ordered his green regiments to make a pivotal attack on the Confederates' right flank on July 3. Stannard lost an arm later in the war.

Dedicated in 1889
39.80943, -77.236336; see map W

VIRGINIA

424. Virginia State Monument

Unveiled on June 8, 1917, the Virginia State Monument honors the state's soldiers who fought at Gettysburg and the men who led them. Virginia was perhaps the most important state of the Confederacy and included its capital, Richmond. The statue of Robert E. Lee and his horse, Traveller, is 14 feet tall and stands atop a 28-foot-tall pedestal. The monument site is in the area where Lee watched Pickett's Charge on July 3.

Dedicated in 1912–1917
39.814255, -77.250473; see map U

WEST VIRGINIA

271. 1ˢᵗ West Virginia Artillery, Battery C (Hill's Battery)

Capt. Wallace Hill commanded Battery C of the 1ˢᵗ West Virginia Light Artillery, part of the Artillery Reserve. When Battery C ran out of ammunition, Battery A of the 1ˢᵗ New Hampshire Light Artillery replaced it in the line. "I think I have just cause to feel proud of the part my men sustained during the entire terrible engagement," Hill reported.

Dedicated in 1898
39.818746, -77.231615; see map N

596. 1ˢᵗ West Virginia Cavalry

The 1ˢᵗ West Virginia Cavalry participated in Gen. Elon Farnsworth's doomed charge on the Union left on July 3. It was "one of the most desperate charges of the present rebellion," in the words of Maj. Charles E. Capehart, who reported five killed and four wounded.

Dedicated in 1898
39.808612, -77.230788; see map W

2. 3ʳᵈ West Virginia Cavalry

Only two companies of the 3ʳᵈ West Virginia Cavalry, a total of 59 men, were at Gettysburg. They served under Capt. Seymour B. Conger.

Dedicated in 1889
39.84355, -77.247916; see map B

240. 7ᵗʰ West Virginia Infantry

The 7ᵗʰ West Virginia belonged to Col. Samuel Carroll's brigade of the 2ⁿᵈ Corps, sent to help repulse the Confederate attack on East Cemetery Hill on the evening of July 2. Moving through the darkness, the Union troops drove back the rebels in furious fighting made all the more confusing by the darkness. In his report Carroll mentioned Lt. Col. Jonathan Lockwood for his "gallant and meritorious conduct on the field."

Dedicated in 1898
39.821712, -77.229018; see map N

291. 7ᵗʰ West Virginia Infantry

The primary monument of the 7ᵗʰ West Virginia is on East Cemetery Hill. This regiment was part of Carroll's brigade of the 2ⁿᵈ Corps. On the night of July 2, the regiment moved forward from this position to help beat back Confederate attacks.

39.815841, -77.232689; see map N

232. 7th West Virginia Infantry

This marker indicates the position of the 7th West Virginia as it pushed attacking rebels back on the evening of July 2.

39.821975, -77.228442; see map N

234. 7th West Virginia Infantry

Another small marker indicates the position of the 7th West Virginia on July 3.

39.82198, -77.227607; see map N

WISCONSIN

91. 2nd Wisconsin Infantry

Then–brigade commander John Gibbon had equipped his men with distinctive high black Hardee hats, headgear from which the Iron Brigade derived its nickname the Black Hat Brigade. There's a carving of a Hardee hat on the 2nd Wisconsin's monument. The regiment led the charge that nabbed Confederate general James Archer, with Pvt. Patrick Mahoney taking credit for the capture.

Dedicated in 1883
39.835664, -77.254059; see map G

316. 2ⁿᵈ Wisconsin Infantry

Following its hard fighting on July 1, the 2ⁿᵈ Wisconsin—one of the regiments of the Iron Brigade—withdrew and established a new position on Culp's Hill. Its primary monument is on Meredith Avenue.

39.8203, -77.222496; see map O

315. Company F, 2ⁿᵈ Wisconsin Infantry

Known as the "Belle City Rifles," Company F of the 2ⁿᵈ Wisconsin Infantry (part of the Iron Brigade) moved here with the other survivors of the regiment after the bloody fighting on July 1.

39.82036, -77.222569; see map O

632. 3ʳᵈ Wisconsin Infantry

The 3ʳᵈ Wisconsin was spared from direct combat during the fighting for Culp's Hill. "Our loss was in skirmishing, not in actual battle," said Lt. Col. George W. Stevenson. "Changed position several times but providentially were saved from the usual slaughter as in other former engagements."

Dedicated in 1888
39.812551, -77.215983; see map Y

846. 5th Wisconsin Infantry

One of the 6th Corps regiments held in reserve, the 5th Wisconsin saw no fighting and suffered no losses at Gettysburg.

Dedicated in 1888
39.783155, -77.2272; see map GG

106. 6th Wisconsin Volunteer Infantry

The 6th Wisconsin was part of the Iron Brigade, as its monument indicates. Under the command of Lt. Col. Rufus Dawes, the 6th Wisconsin participated in the battle for the railroad cut, moving forward "under a most destructive fire of musketry." The Confederates in the cut discovered that the "steep, rocky sides afforded no opportunity for escape after they were once penned up in it."

Dedicated in 1888
39.837395, -77.248213; see map G

317. 6th Wisconsin Infantry

The 6th Wisconsin fell back from the fighting north of town on July 1. "The morning of the second day found us lying quietly in the breastworks near the summit of Culp's Hill," remembered Lt. Col. Rufus Dawes. This small marker indicates that position.

39.820164, -77.221613; see map O

90. 7th Wisconsin Infantry

One of the regiments of the all-western Iron Brigade, the 7th Wisconsin charged across Willoughby Run with the 2nd Wisconsin in the action that captured Archer's brigade on July 1. Lt. Col. John Callis recalled giving the order to fix bayonets "and away we went depending on cold steel." Callis also said he gave John Burns the rifle the old man used in place of his musket.

Dedicated in 1888
39.835764, -77.253807; see map G

314. 7th Wisconsin Infantry

The 7th Wisconsin, part of the Iron Brigade, had fought hard on July 1 (its main monument is on Meredith Avenue). It fell back through town and on to Culp's Hill.

39.819697, -77.223287; see map O

59. 26th Wisconsin Infantry

One soldier from the 26th Wisconsin said "the bullets came thick as hail" before the regiment retreated through Gettysburg on July 1. "It seemed so awful to march back through those same streets whipped and beaten," wrote another soldier.

Dedicated in 1888
39.843412, -77.229357; see map D

483. Wisconsin Sharpshooters (Company G, 1st United States Sharpshooters)

One company of Col. Hiram Berdan's regiment of sharpshooters, the Wisconsin Sharpshooters were placed on picket duty on the morning of July 2. The company fell back with the rest of the 3rd Corps that afternoon under the pressure of the Confederate attack. There's also a position marker in the field beyond the monument.

Dedicated in 1888
39.808081, -77.244348; see map V

480. Wisconsin Sharpshooters

This small marker shows the position of Company G of the 1st United States Sharpshooters, also known as the Wisconsin Sharpshooters, on July 2. The company's monument is about 200 yards to the east on the Emmitsburg Road.

39.80946, -77.245827; see map V

PEOPLE

527. Brig. Gen. Lewis Armistead

One of the iconic images from Gettysburg is that of Lewis Armistead lifting his black hat high on the point of his sword as he led his surviving men across the stone wall at the climax of Pickett's Charge. Armistead fell mortally wounded. Born in North Carolina, Armistead had been kicked out of West Point after he broke a plate over the head of Jubal Early, another future Confederate general. This was Gettysburg's first monument to a fallen Confederate officer.

Dedicated in 1887
39.813066, -77.235938; see map W

65. Maj. Gen. Francis Barlow

When war broke out, Francis Barlow was a Harvard graduate practicing law in New York. He joined the army as a private. A strict disciplinarian, Barlow was brave and aggressive—perhaps too aggressive. As the commander of the 11th Corps' 1st Division he moved his men to the knoll that now bears his name, overextending the Union line. Badly wounded at Gettysburg, Barlow recovered to lead a division in the 2nd Corps.

Dedicated in 1922
39.845411, -77.226426; see map D

78. Maj. Gen. John Buford

Tough and efficient, cavalryman John Buford performed invaluable service by delaying the Confederate advance on July 1. He was described as "a compactly built man of middle height, with a tawny moustache and a little, triangular gray eye, whose expression is determined, not to say sinister." Buford died of typhoid fever in December 1863. Surrounding his statue's base are four cannon, one of which supposedly fired the first artillery round of the battle.

Dedicated in 1895 or 1892
39.837928, -77.251638; see map G

"The enemy's force (A. P. Hill's) are advancing on me at this point and driving my pickets and skirmishers very rapidly. There is also a large force at Heidlersburg, that is driving my pickets at that point from that direction. General Reynolds is advancing, and is within three miles of this point, with his leading division. I am positive that the whole of A. P. Hill's force is advancing."

—message sent by Brig. Gen. John Buford to Maj. Gen. Meade at 10:10 a.m. on July 1

88. John Burns

Eccentric John Burns, "The Old Hero of Gettysburg," was nearly 70 when the contending armies reached Gettysburg. He grabbed his musket and headed out to shoot some "damned Rebels." The colonel of the 150th Pennsylvania advised Burns to move into the woods with the Iron Brigade. There he fought "as cool as if standing in a field shooting at birds" until he was wounded three times. After the battle, he became a celebrity.

Dedicated in 1902–1903
39.835886, -77.252799; see map G

710. Capt. Jedediah Chapman

Jedediah Chapman was commanding the 27th Connecticut's Company H when he fell near this spot on July 2. "He was one of the most unassuming of men, and yet in that soul burned a depth of devotion to duty, and a power of noble action, which seemed to require the stern, trying scenes of war to bring them forth in their original strength, and glory," said a regimental history.

39.796251, -77.245487; see map BB

264. Bvt. Maj. Gen. Charles H. Collis

Irish-born Charles H. Collis was the colonel of the 114th Pennsylvania, known as Collis's Zouaves. Collis, who earned the Medal of Honor for his actions at Fredericksburg, was wounded at Chancellorsville, and became ill with typhoid fever so he missed the fighting at Gettysburg. He moved to the town after the war and his house, which he called Red Patch for the insignia of his division of the 3rd Corps, still stands on West Confederate Avenue.

Dedicated in 1906
39.819918, -77.232001; see map N

> *"The handful of men, before going into that fierce battle, knelt down; the excellent chaplain, Father Corby, piously raised his hands, and gave them his benediction. They then jumped to their feet, closed up their lines, and charged."*
>
> —From *The Irish Brigade and its Campaigns* by Thomas Conyngham

618. Father William Corby

Father William Corby was the chaplain for the famed Irish Brigade of the Army of the Potomac's 2nd Corps. On July 2, before the brigade prepared to go into battle in the Wheatfield, Father Corby stood on this rock and gave absolution to the soldiers kneeling before him. After the war the "Fighting Chaplain" became president of the University of Notre Dame. Sculptor Samuel Murray also created the Goddess of Victory and Peace that tops the Pennsylvania State Monument.

Dedicated in 1910
39.803519, -77.234302; see map W

731. Brig. Gen. Samuel Crawford

Pennsylvanian Samuel Crawford began the war as an army surgeon at Fort Sumter and ended it as a division commander at Appomattox. In between he became the commander of the Pennsylvania Reserves. At one point during the Reserves' charge here, Crawford, on horseback, took the division flag from a flag-bearer, who trotted alongside the general until he gave it back. Sculptor Ron Tunison also did the Delaware State and Friend to Friend Masonic Monuments and the Elizabeth Thorn bronze in Evergreen Cemetery.

Dedicated in 1988
39.795951, -77.23879; see map BB

530. Lt. Alonzo H. Cushing

Lt. Alonzo H. Cushing commanded the 4th U.S. Battery of the 2nd Corps artillery reserve. Badly wounded by Confederate artillery in the prelude to Pickett's Charge, he remained with his two remaining guns at the stone wall until he received a final, fatal wound in the mouth. The Wisconsin native was only 22.

Dedicated in 1887
39.813108, -77.235686; see map W

118. Maj. Gen. Abner Doubleday

Born in 1819 in Ballston Spa, New York, Abner Doubleday was at Fort Sumter and may have fired the first Union shot of the war. At Gettysburg, he assumed command of the 1st Corps after Reynolds died. He performed well, but Gen. Meade replaced him with John Newton. Doubleday never forgave the perceived slight and saw no more active service during the war. He later became famous for inventing baseball—something he didn't do.

Dedicated in 1917
39.833015, -77.25076; see map G

344. Brig. Gen. John Geary

Before the Civil War, John Geary fought in Mexico and served as San Francisco's first mayor and as territorial governor of "Bleeding Kansas." When war came, he raised the 28th Pennsylvania and fought well at Cedar Mountain and Chancellorsville. A big man—he stood 6 feet 6 inches—Geary unfortunately got lost on July 2 when sent to reinforce the Union left. He ended the war as a major general and served two terms as Pennsylvania's governor.

Dedicated in 1914
39.81731, -77.219886; see map O

555. Brig. Gen. John Gibbon

Born in Philadelphia, John Gibbon grew up in North Carolina. He remained loyal to the Union, however (though three of his brothers joined the Confederates). At Gettysburg, he led the 2nd Division of the 2nd Corps. He was wounded on July 3, but ended the war in command of a corps. One of Gen. Meade's staffers later described Gibbon as "a tower of strength . . . cool as a steel knife, always, and unmoved by anything and everything."

Dedocated om 1988
39.810976, -77.235406; see map W

325. Brig. Gen. George S. Greene

At 62, George Sears Greene was the oldest general—perhaps the oldest soldier—at Gettysburg. He provided invaluable service after most of the 12th Corps was sent to support the Union left, leaving only the five regiments of Greene's brigade to defend the Union right at Culp's Hill. Fortunately, Greene insisted on having his troops construct breastworks, despite division commander John Geary's opinion that it would prove detrimental to their fighting ability.

Dedicated in 1906
39.819874, -77.220079; see map O

> *"Greene's brigade, of the Second Division, remained in the intrenchments, and the failure of the enemy to gain entire possession of our works was due entirely to the skill of General Greene and the heroic valor of his troops. His brigade suffered severely, but maintained its position, and held the enemy in check until the return of Williams' division."*
>
> —Maj. Gen. Henry Slocum to Maj. Gen. George Meade, December 30, 1863

> *The enemy was emerging from the streets of the town below, and form-ing line as if to charge and drive us from our coveted position. Every man knew how hopeless resistance would be, but Hancock sat his horse, superb and calm as on review; imperturbable, self-reliant, as if the fate of the battle and of the nation were not his to decide. It almost led us to doubt whether there had been cause for retreat at all."*
>
> —Lt. Sidney G. Cooke, 147th New York Infantry, about
> the Union recovery on Cemetery Hill on July 1

255. Maj. Gen. Winfield Scott Hancock

Nicknamed "the Superb" for his actions outside Richmond in 1862, Winfield Scott Hancock rose to command the Army of the Potomac's 2nd Corps. After John Reynolds' death, Gen. Meade sent Hancock to Gettys-burg to take command there. He helped steady the men on Cemetery Hill on July 1 and performed admirably on July 2 and 3, but was badly wounded during the repulse of Pickett's Charge. Hancock was the Demo-cratic nominee for president in 1880.

Dedicated in 1895
39.821265, -77.228929; see map N

573. Site of Maj. Gen. Winfield Scott Hancock's Wounding

Maj. Gen. Winfield Scott Hancock per-formed Herculean labors at Gettysburg until he was wounded on July 3 during the climax of the fighting. A bullet ripped through his saddle and into his groin, carry-ing a saddle nail into the wound. Hancock survived to rejoin the army for the Overland Campaign in 1864, but his wound contin-ued to trouble him throughout the war.

Dedicated in 1886–1893
39.808886, -77.237015; see map W

283. Brig. Gen. Alexander Hays

Born in Franklin, Pennsylvania, Alexander Hays was in command of the 2nd Corps' 3rd Division at Gettysburg. He was brave and profane and, after the repulse of Pickett's Charge, delighted his men by dragging a captured flag behind his horse. His courage during the cannonade prompted one of his soldiers to say, "I think he is the bravest division general I ever saw in the saddle." Hays died in the Battle of the Wilderness on May 5, 1864.

Dedicated in 1915
39.816831, -77.234597; see map N

231. Maj. Gen. Oliver O. Howard

Born in Maine in 1830, Oliver O. Howard graduated from Bowdoin College and West Point. He lost his right arm in the 1862 Richmond campaign. At Chancellorsville, his 11th Corps broke under Stonewall Jackson's flank attack; at Gettysburg it broke again on July 1. Howard ended the war fighting under Sherman. A pious man (his troops called him "Old Prayer Book"), he headed the Freedmen's Bureau after the war. Howard University in Washington, DC, is named after him.

39.82196, -77.2289; see map N

WHAT WAS PICKETT'S CHARGE?

The Confederate attack on Cemetery Ridge on July 3, 1863, is popularly remembered as Pickett's Charge. Historians often take issue with the name—Confederate general George Pickett led only one of the three divisions that took part in the attack, with the other two commanded by Brig. Gen. James Pettigrew and Brig. Gen. Isaac Trimble, so a more accurate name would be the Pickett-Pettigrew-Trimble Assault. Others say it should be named after James Longstreet, the 1st Corps commander who was given overall responsibility for the assault (though he argued against making it). But the attack has come to be remembered as Pickett's Charge nonetheless.

481. Brig. Gen. Andrew A. Humphreys

Philadelphian Andrew A. Humphreys commanded a division in the 3rd Corps and held the right of Sickles's advanced position. "He was a small, bow-legged man, with chopped-off, iron gray moustache," a staff member recalled. "His blue-gray dauntless eyes threw into his stern face the coldness of hammered steel." Assistant secretary of war Charles Dana said Humphreys "was one of the loudest swearers that I ever knew." After the battle he became Meade's chief of staff.

Dedicated in 1914
39.808202, -77.243856; see map V

440. Lt. Gen. James Longstreet

Robert E. Lee once called Lt. Gen. James Longstreet his "old war horse." Longstreet commanded the Army of Virginia's 1st Corps and after the war was dogged by accusations that his sluggishness on July 2 lost the battle for the Confederacy. He also resisted Lee's plans to attack the Union center on July 3. That helps explain why Longstreet did not get a statue at Gettysburg until 1998.

Dedicated in 1998
39.805774, -77.256565; see map U

I have been in pretty much all kinds of skirmishes, from those of two or three soldiers up to those of an army corps, and I think I can safely say there never was a body of fifteen thousand men who could make that attack successfully."

—Lt. Gen. James Longstreet, arguing with Lee about the futility of attacking Cemetery Ridge on July 3

293. Maj. Gen. George Gordon Meade

Promoted to command the Army of the Potomac on June 28, only three days before the Battle of Gettysburg, George Meade ably led his forces to the first major victory over the Army of Northern Virginia. Born in Cadiz, Spain, where his father served as a naval agent, Meade was wounded during the Peninsula Campaign and rose from command of a brigade, to a division, to the 5th Corps. He retained command of the army until the war ended, although general-in-chief Ulysses S. Grant accompanied the army in the field. Meade died in 1872 and is buried in Philadelphia.

Dedicated in 1895
39.813902, -77.23474; see map N

681. Lt. Col. Henry Mervin

This small marker along Wheatfield Road marks the spot where the commander of the 27th Connecticut fell during the fighting on July 2. The regiment's monument is nearby.

39.797581, -77.240831; see map BB

213. John Page Nicholson

Philadelphia bookbinder John Pace Nicholson served in the 28th Pennsylvania Infantry from July 20, 1861, until he was mustered out in July 1865. He served as chairman of the Gettysburg National Park Commission from 1893 to 1922.

Dedicated in 1922
39.814621, -77.23529; see map M

322. Maj. J. G. Putnam

Maj. Joshua G. Putnam was with the 66th Ohio when he fell mortally wounded on this spot on July 3.

39.820127, -77.219404; see map O

396. Bvt. Lt. Col. Brooke Rawle Flagpole

William Brooke Rawle was a 19-year-old lieutenant with the 3rd Pennsylvania Cavalry, who fought here on July 3. After the war, Rawle wrote books about cavalry operations during the Gettysburg campaign.

39.827746, -77.168185; see map R

82. Maj. Gen. John Fulton Reynolds

Born in Lancaster, Pennsylvania, John Fulton Reynolds graduated from West Point in 1841. After Chancellorsville, president Lincoln sounded him out about commanding the Army of the Potomac. Reynolds declined. Gen. Meade put him in charge of the army's left wing at Gettysburg, and a Confederate bullet killed him on the morning of July 1. "His look and manner denoted uncommon coolness," said one of his officers; another called him "a type of the true soldier."

Dedicated in 1899
39.837891, -77.251286; see map G

237. Maj. Gen. John Fulton Reynolds

This statue to John Fulton Reynolds, who was killed in fighting on July 1, was one of the first monuments erected on the Gettysburg Battlefield. The metal came from Civil War cannons. Reynolds, from Lancaster, Pennsylvania, also has a statute on Chambersburg Pike and a likeness on the Pennsylvania Memorial. A monument off Reynolds Avenue indicates the spot where he was killed.

Dedicated in 1871
39.821216, -77.230242; see map N

115. Death of Maj. Gen. John Fulton Reynolds

"Forward, men, forward for God's sake, and drive those fellows out of the woods," shouted Maj. Gen. John Reynolds as he positioned the men of the Iron Brigade on July 1. He looked behind him, and a Confederate bullet struck him in the back of the neck. He was the highest-ranking officer to die here. There are two other monuments to Reynolds at Gettysburg, on Chambersburg Pike and in the National Cemetery.

Dedicated in 1886
39.834028, -77.251002; see map G

"When near the town I met Captain Mitchell with an ambulance, and General Reynolds's body. I felt very badly indeed about his death, as he had always treated me very kindly, and because he was the best general we had in our army. Brave, kind-hearted, modest, somewhat rough and wanting polish, he was a type of the true soldier. I cannot realize that he is dead. The last time I saw him he was alive and well, and now to think of him as dead seems an impossibility."

—Capt. Steven M. Weld

25. Brig. Gen. John Cleveland Robinson

Born in Binghamton, New York, in 1817, John Cleveland Robinson entered West Point in 1835 but was expelled before he could graduate. Nonetheless he joined the army and served in Mexico. He commanded the garrison at Baltimore's Fort McHenry when war broke out. At Gettysburg, he commanded the 2nd Division of the 1st Corps. Although outnumbered, his men delayed the Confederate advance on July 1. Robinson lost a leg outside Spotsylvania Court House in 1864 and died in 1897.

Dedicated in 1917
39.843439, -77.241981; see map B

785. Maj. Gen. John Sedgwick

Maj. Gen. John Sedgwick was loved by his men, who called him "Uncle John." The Connecticut native was dependable although cautious. Sedgwick's corps made a brutal forced march of 36 miles to reach the Gettysburg Battlefield. Gen. Meade threw elements of the 6th Corps into battle piecemeal, until Sedgwick complained he no longer had any men to command. He was killed by a Confederate sharpshooter's bullet at Spotsylvania Court House on May 9, 1864.

Dedicated in 1913
39.796184, -77.234151; see map CC

> *"One of the best generals we had: a man of utterly transparent honesty, simplicity, and truth of character; trusted, beloved, ardently followed by his men; a commander who had done great things and was capable of greater."*
>
> —War correspondent George Smalley about Maj. Gen. John Sedgwick

516. Maj. Gen. Daniel E. Sickles

General Daniel Sickles was controversial—before the war, he had killed his wife's lover; during the battle, he moved his 3rd Corps forward without orders. He was mounted on his horse near the Trostle barn on July 2 when a cannonball hit his leg. According to legend, Sickles calmly smoked a cigar as he was removed from the battlefield, to keep his men from panicking. A surgeon removed the leg, which went on display at the Army Medical Museum. Sickles visited it every year.

39.802587, -77.242794; see map V

311. Maj. Gen. Henry W. Slocum

12th Corps commander Maj. Gen. Henry W. Slocum commanded the Union's right wing at Gettysburg. Born in 1827 in Delphi, New York, he graduated from West Point in 1852 and practiced law before the war. Slocum was wounded at First Bull Run; at Gettysburg he earned the nickname "Slow Come" because he dallied on July 1 rather than become senior commander on the field. Slocum later fought under Sherman.

Dedicated in 1902
39.819203, -77.224537; see map O

729. Col. Charles F. Taylor, 13th Pennsylvania Reserves Infantry

Col. Charles F. Taylor, the 23-year-old commander of the Bucktails (13th Pennsylvania Reserves), fell to a Confederate bullet in the breast as he was preparing to order up more men for an assault on the rebels at Devil's Den. "Probably no officer of the Bucktails was ever better or more generally loved than Colonel Taylor," read a history of the regiment.

Dedicated in 1905
39.79566, -77.241236; see map BB

809. Brig. Gen. Strong Vincent

Harvard graduate and lawyer Strong Vincent had been recently promoted to brigade command. On July 2, he brought his troops to Little Round Top and quickly placed them in position, the 20th Maine on the left and the 16th Michigan on the right. He was mortally wounded while directing the defense. "This is the fourth or fifth time they have shot at me, and they have hit me at last," he reportedly said. This is a replacement for the original stone, which was broken.

Dedicated in 1878
39.790923, -77.237163; see map CC

101. Brig. Gen. James Samuel Wadsworth

Brig. Gen. James Samuel Wadsworth (1807-64) came from wealth and privilege but volunteered as an aide to Gen. Irvin McDowell and later commanded one of his brigades. In 1862, he ran (unsuccessfully) for governor of New York. His division of the 1st Corps was the first infantry to reach John Buford's cavalry on July 1, and it suffered heavily. Wadsworth was mortally wounded in the Battle of the Wilderness.

Dedicated in 1914
39.838251, -77.247782; see map G

472. Col. George H. Ward (15th Massachusetts Infantry)

Col. George H. Ward of the 15th Massachusetts had lost a leg at the Battle of Ball's Bluff in 1861. He returned to duty in February 1863. At Gettysburg, on July 2, his regiment advanced on the left of the 2nd Corps to fill a gap in the line. Forced to withdraw under heavy fire—some of which came from the Union cannon to the rear—Ward fell mortally wounded.

39.812347, -77.239003; see map V

800. Maj. Gen. G. K. Warren

Gouverneur Kemble Warren was born in New York state and graduated second in the West Point class of 1850. He had commanded a regiment and a brigade before becoming the army's chief engineer. At Gettysburg, Brig. Gen. Warren recognized the importance of Little Round Top and, on July 2, rushed Union soldiers there to defend it. It was his finest hour. He later commanded the 5th Corps, until Philip Sheridan relieved him of command at Five Forks.

Dedicated in 1888
39.792562, -77.236622; see map CC

534. Brig. Gen. Alexander Webb

Promoted to brigadier general on June 23 and given command of the Philadelphia Brigade only days before the battle, Brig. Gen. Alexander Webb found his new command facing the spear point of Pickett's Charge at the Angle on Cemetery Ridge. Although initially distrustful of their new commander, the brigade found reason to salute his leadership and courage. Webb later won the Medal of Honor for his actions here.

Dedicated in 1915
39.81298, -77.235389; see map W

"General Armistead (an old army officer) led his men, came over my fence and passed me with four men. He fell mortally wounded. . . . When they were over the fence the Army of the Potomac was nearer being whipped than it was at any time of the battle."

—Brig. Gen. Alexander Webb, writing to his wife about the climax of Pickett's Charge

828. Maj. William Wells, 1st Vermont Cavalry

Maj. Williams Wells led four companies of cavalry in the doomed charge ordered on July 3 by Judson Kilpatrick and led by Elon Farnsworth. "It was a swift resistless charge over rocks, through timber, under close enfilading fire." Unlike Farnsworth, Wells survived the attack (depicted on the monument's bas-relief) and later earned the Medal of Honor for his actions.

Dedicated in 1913
39.784807, -77.245576; see map EE

803. Hazlett-Weed Memorial

Formerly the 91st Pennsylvania's monument, this monument now honors artilleryman Capt. Charles Hazlett and Brig. Gen. Steven Weed, both of whom died here. Weed was struck down by a Confederate bullet and Hazlett, after having his battery hauled to the top of Little Round Top, was mortally wounded trying to hear Weed's last words.

39.792115, -77.236662; see map CC

680. Brig. Gen. Samuel Kosciusko Zook

Gen. Samuel K. Zook remained mounted as he advanced his brigade of the 2nd Corps into the Wheatfield on July 2. A Confederate bullet hit him in the stomach. "It's all up with me, Favill," he told the lieutenant who came to his aid. Zook, a Pennsylvanian, was right. He died on July 3. The monument was fashioned from marble from Zook's father's farm.

Dedicated in 1882
39.798358, -77.242555; see map BB

GETTYSBURG NATIONAL MILITARY PARK

Gettysburg was not the first battlefield to become a national park—it was the fourth (Chickamauga/Chattanooga, Antietam, and Shiloh preceded it). Congressman Daniel Sickles, the Union 3rd Corps commander who had lost his leg in the battle, introduced legislation to have the Gettysburg battlefield turned into a national park in December 1894, and President Grover Cleveland signed the bill creating the Gettysburg National Military Park on February 11, 1895. The park included 800 acres handed over by the Gettysburg Battlefield Memorial Association, with boundaries based on a map that Sickles had drawn. The U.S. War Department had jurisdiction over the park until the National Park Service took responsibility in 1933.

MONUMENTS TO THE UNION ARMY

781. 5th Army Corps

When Daniel Butterfield, chief of staff to Army of the Potomac commander Joseph Hooker, designed distinctive badges for each army corps, he gave the 5th Corps a Maltese Cross. Maj. Gen. George Sykes commanded the 5th Corps at Gettysburg, after taking over from George Meade when Meade received command of the army.

Dedicated in 1898
39.797073, -77.234271; see map CC

201. Grand Army of the Republic (Alfred Woolson)

Membership in the Grand Army of the Republic was restricted to honorably discharged Union veterans; at one point it had nearly half a million members. Alfred Woolson, its last surviving member, died in 1956 at the age of 109.

Dedicated in 1956
39.816059, -77.234938; see map M

552. United States Regular Army

Most of the soldiers fighting for the Union were volunteers, raised by the states. Members of the Regular Army, the professional soldiers of the federal government, made up only about 8 percent of the forces at Gettysburg, or 7,176 men. Their monument is 85 feet high.

Dedicated on May 31, 1909
39.811286, -77.235839; see map W

MONUMENTS TO THE CONFEDERATE ARMY

824. Soldiers and Sailors of the Confederacy Monument

Occupying a plot of land that was once supposed to contain a statue of Gen. James Longstreet, the Soldiers and Sailors of the Confederacy Monument honors all those who fought for the Confederacy. Sculptor Donald DeLue also created the monuments for Louisiana and Mississippi. On the base is the name of Walter Washington Williams, supposedly the last surviving Confederate veteran, although there are questions about that claim.

Dedicated on May 18, 1905
39.784966, -77.254066; see map EE

> *"The conduct of the troops was all that I could desire or expect, and they deserve success so far as it can be deserved by heroic valor and fortitude. More may have been required of them than they were able to perform."*
>
> —Gen. Robert E. Lee in his official report on the Gettysburg campaign

OTHER

402. Cavalry Shaft

The Cavalry Shaft memorializes the fighting that took place here on July 3, when Confederate cavalry under Jeb Stuart attempted to circle around to attack the rear of the Army of the Potomac. Union cavalry under Brig. Gen. David McMurtrie Gregg stopped them. "The losses on both sides show the importance and determined character of the fight," wrote one participant.

Dedicated in 1884
39.826409, -77.163132; see map S

12. Eternal Light Peace Memorial

President Franklin Roosevelt dedicated the Eternal Light Peace Memorial on July 3, 1938, the battle's 75th anniversary. Some 250,000 people were present, including around 1,800 elderly Gettysburg veterans. The 40-foot shaft of Alabama limestone stands on a base of Maine granite and is topped by a torch fueled by natural gas (replaced by electricity for a time before being restored in 1988). The words "Peace Eternal in a Nation United" are engraved across the monument's base.

Dedicated on July 3, 1938
39.848419, -77.243539; see map B

> "Men who wore the blue and men who wore the gray are here together, a fragment spared by time. They are brought here by the memories of old divided loyalties, but they meet here in united loyalty to a united cause which the unfolding years have made it easier to see."
>
> —President Franklin D. Roosevelt at the dedication of the Eternal Light Peace Memorial, July 3, 1938

261. Friend to Friend Masonic Memorial

Sculpted by Ron Tunison, who also did the statue of Samuel Crawford and the Delaware State Monument, the Friend to Friend Masonic Memorial depicts Confederate general Lewis Armistead as he lay dying at the close of the Confederate attack on July 3. The mortally wounded Armistead, a Mason, gave his personal effects to Union captain Henry Bingham and asked that they be returned to his family.

Dedicated in 1994–1995
39.820983, -77.23201; see map N

43. Gettysburg Battlefield Preservation Association (1965)

This tablet was dedicated on November 19, 1965.

Dedicated in 1965
39.840573, -77.235557; see map C

253. Gettysburg Women's Memorial

Elizabeth Thorn was the wife of Evergreen Cemetery's caretaker, who was in the army. After enduring an artillery barrage along with 16 other people crammed into the basement, she was evicted from her home in the cemetery's gatehouse. She returned to find a wasteland. She then buried more than 100 soldiers. Thorn was six months pregnant at the time. (She named her daughter Rose Meade, after the victor of Gettysburg.)

39.820579, -77.229359; see map N

539. The High Water Mark of the Rebellion

Designed by John B. Bachelder, an artist who became an early and pivotal battlefield historian, this bronze book of history stands by the Copse of Trees and the furthest advance of Pickett's Charge. It lists all the commands involved in the attack; before its dedication it was discovered that two were missing, and the monument had to be recast.

Dedicated on June 2, 1892
39.812593, -77.23578; see map W

276. Lincoln Address Memorial

President Abraham Lincoln made his Gettysburg Address at the dedication of the National Cemetery on November 19, 1863. The spot where he spoke is believed to be near the Soldiers National Monument. The headliner was former Harvard president Edward Everett. "I should be glad, if I could flatter myself that I came as near to the central idea of the occasion, in two hours, as you did in two minutes," Everett wrote the president.

Dedicated on January 24, 1912
39.817503, -77.231907; see map N

97. MOLLUS Monument

A marker commemorating a donation of 12,265 acres of land donated by the War Library and Museum and Pennsylvania Commandery of the Military Order of the Loyal Legion of the United States (MOLLUS).

Dedicated in 1963
39.83912, -77.247479; see map G

99. MOLLUS Monument

Another MOLLUS commemorative marker, this one for the donation of 7.45 acres.

Dedicated in 1963
39.839004, -77.247124; see map G

210. Pettigrew's Charge

This marker indicates the aiming point of the division led by Brig. Gen. James Johnston Pettigrew, commanding in place of the wounded Harry Heth. He had 4,570 men. Pickett's division, with 5,043 men, advanced to Pettigrew's left, with the 2,200 men of the division under Brig. Gen. Isaac Trimble (replacing a mortally wounded William Pender) following.

39.814799, -77.235503; see map M

266. Soldiers National Monument

This is the battlefield's first monument—the cornerstone was laid on July 4, 1865, and the monument itself was dedicated on July 1, 1869. The four statues around the base represent War, History, Plenty, and Peace. Standing atop the 60-foot column is "the Genius of Liberty." Randolph Rogers was the sculptor and James Goodwin Batterson and George W. Keller the designers.

Dedicated on July 1, 1869
39.819789, -77.231284; see map N

"For two hours the roar was continuous and loud as that from the falls of Niagara."

—Col. Charles S. Wainwright, artillery chief for the Union
1st Corps, about the artillery bombardment on July 3

643. Spangler Farm/Armistead and Hancock

This small marker on Blacksmith Shop Road is near the Spangler Farm, near the places where Confederate Brigadier Generals Lewis Armistead and Union Major General Winfield Scott Hancock were treated for their wounds. Armistead died but Hancock survived. The two men had been close friends before the war.

39.80118; -77.212825; see map Y

371. Spangler's Spring

Legend says that Union and Confederate soldiers honored unofficial truces so both sides could refill their canteens at Spangler's Spring, which lay between the lines during the battle. Although a nice story, it appears to have no basis in fact. Another legend says the ghost of a woman in white haunts the spring today.

39.814571, -77.217329; see map O

LINCOLN'S GETTYSBURG ADDRESS
NOVEMBER 19, 1863

Four score and seven years ago our fathers brought forth on this continent, a new nation, conceived in Liberty, and dedicated to the proposition that all men are created equal.

Now we are engaged in a great civil war, testing whether that nation, or any nation so conceived and so dedicated, can long endure. We are met on a great battle-field of that war. We have come to dedicate a portion of that field, as a final resting place for those who here gave their lives that that nation might live. It is altogether fitting and proper that we should do this.

But, in a larger sense, we can not dedicate, we can not consecrate, we can not hallow this ground. The brave men, living and dead, who struggled here, have consecrated it, far above our poor power to add or detract. The world will little note, nor long remember what we say here, but it can never forget what they did here. It is for us the living, rather, to be dedicated here to the unfinished work which they who fought here have thus far so nobly advanced. It is rather for us to be here dedicated to the great task remaining before us—that from these honored dead we take increased devotion to that cause for which they gave the last full measure of devotion—that we here highly resolve that these dead shall not have died in vain—that this nation, under God, shall have a new birth of freedom—and that government of the people, by the people, for the people, shall not perish from the earth.

TABLETS AND MARKERS

ALABAMA

10. Hardaway's Alabama Artillery (39.84888, -77.24369; see map B)
137. Hardaway's Alabama Artillery (39.828118, -77.2447; see map H)
18. Jeff Davis Rifles (Reese's Battery) (39.847328, -77.242008; see map B)
813. Law's Brigade, Hood's Division, 1st Corps (39.789618, -77.237439; see map CC)
820. Law's Brigade, Hood's Division, 1st Corps (39.787082, -77.25412; see map EE)
19. O'Neal's Brigade (39.846144, -77.242452; see map B)
308. O'Neal's Brigade, Rodes' Division, 2nd Corps (39.819735, -77.216703; see map O)
494. Wilcox's Brigade, Anderson's Division, 3rd Corps (39.805175, -77.245996; see map V)
434. Wilcox's Brigade, Anderson's Division, 3rd Corps (39.808638, -77.255135; see map U)

GEORGIA

158. Georgia Artillery (39.829591, -77.212803; see map K)
185. Lane's Battalion, Anderson's Division, 3rd Corps (39.818775, -77.247497; see map L)
438. Patterson's Battery (39.806409, -77.256368; see map U)
665. Pulaski Artillery, Cabell's Battalion, McLaw's Division (39.795106, -77.25528; see map AA)
182. Ross's Battery (Battery A), the Sumter Artillery (39.819549, -77.247092; see map L)
655. Semmes' Brigade, McLaw's Division, 1st Corps (39.79874, -77.255967; see map AA)
716. Semmes' Brigade, McLaw's Division, 1st Corps (39.795035, -77.247125; see map BB)

662. Troup Artillery, 1st Section (39.797278; -77.255585; see map AA)
653. Troup Artillery, 2nd Section (Carlton's Battery) (39.799025, -77.256024; see map AA)
188. Wingfield's Battery (Battery C), the Sumter Artillery (39.818489, -77.24784; see map L)
469. Wofford's Brigade, McLaw's Division, 1st Corps (39.800672, -77.250608; see map U)
447. Wofford's Brigade, McLaw's Division, 1st Corps (39.803192, -77.256057; see map U)
544. Wright's Brigade, Anderson's Division, 3rd Corps (39.811971, -77.236761; see map W)
426. Wright's Brigade, Anderson's Division, 3rd Corps (39.814109, -77.250875; see map U)

LOUISIANA

166. Donaldsonville Artillery (Maurin's Battery) (39.826149, -77.244875; see map L)
448. Eshelman's Artillery Battalion, McLaw's Division, 1st Corps (39.803137, -77.256017; see map U)
153. Hay's Brigade, Early's Division, 2nd Corps (39.828784, -77.226299; see map J)
76. Louisiana Guard Artillery (39.851626, -77.213074; see map E)
384. Louisiana Guard Artillery (39.838257, -77.167237; see map R)
454. Madison Light Artillery (39.801851, -77.256153; see map U)
306. Nicholl's Brigade, Johnson's Division, 2nd Corps (39.821146, -77.217673; see map O)
445. Norcom's Battery (39.804012, -77.25602; see map U)
446. Richardson's Battery (39.803419, -77.256002; see map U)
451. Squires' Battery (39.802766, -77.256094; see map U)

MARYLAND

163. 1st Maryland Battery (39.826822, -77.213956; see map K)
160. Chesapeake, Maryland, Artillery (39.8285, -77.213309; see map K)

MASSACHUSETTS

607. 5th Massachusetts Artillery, Battery E (39.80569, -77.23481; see map W)
839. Massachusetts Light Artillery, Battery C (39.784877, -77.231696; see map GG)

MISSISSIPPI

450. Barksdale's Brigade, McLaw's Division, 1st Corps (39.802833, -77.256126; see map U)

462. Barksdale's Brigade, McLaw's Division, 1st Corps (39.801446, -77.250281; see map U)

421. Posey's Brigade, Anderson's Division, 3rd Corps (39.814594, -77.250514; see map U)

423. Madison Mississippi Light Artillery (39.814525, -77.250388; see map U)

NEW JERSEY

614. 1st New Jersey Light Artillery, Battery B (Clark's Battery) (39.804326, -77.23465; see map W)

613. 2nd Battery, New Jersey Light Artillery (39.804351, -77.234653; see map W)

NEW YORK

842. 1st New York Light Artillery, Battery C (39.783687, -77.22897; see map GG)

745. 4th New York Independent Battery (39.794304, -77.23982; see map BB)

251. 5th New York Independent Battery (39.820637, -77.229699; see map N)

610. 15th Battery, New York Light Artillery (39.805181, -77.234745; see map W)

NORTH CAROLINA

657. 1st North Carollina Artillery (39.798157, -77.255869; see map AA)

416. Albermarle Artillery (39.817524, -77.248274; see map U)

671. Branch Artilllery (Latham's Battery), Henry's Battalion (39.790415, -77.254328; see map AA)

192. Charlotte Artillery (39.818035, -77.248059; see map L)

11. Daniel's Brigade (39.848728, -77.243581; see map B)

309. Daniel's Brigade (39.819069, -77.216182; see map O)

154. Hoke's Brigade, Early's Division, 2nd Corps (39.827959, -77.225616; see map J)

15. Iverson's Brigade (39.847912, -77.243131; see map B)

415. Pettigrew's Brigade, Heth's Division, 3rd Corps (39.81758, -77.248362; see map U)

8. Ramseur's Brigade (39.848178, -77.244729; see map B)

823. Rowan Artillery (39.785203, -77.254132; see map EE)

825. Rowan Artillery (39.784338; -77.252427; see map EE)

OHIO

249. 1st Ohio Artillery, Battery I (39.820986, -77.229826; see map N)

848. 5th Ohio Infantry (39.794480, -77.234617; see map CC)

PENNSYLVANIA

233. 1st Pennsylvania Light Artillery, Battery B (39.82175, -77.228676; see map N)

606. 1st Pennsylvania Light Artillery Battery B (39.806169, -77.234892; see map W)

611. 3rd Pennsylvania Heavy Artillery, Battery H (39.80488, -77.234711; see map W)

SOUTH CAROLINA

850. Brooks Artillery (39.80243, -77.25601; see map U)

676. German Artillery (39.789018, -77.253842; see map AA)

659. Kershaw's Brigade, McLaw's Division, 1st Corps (39.798261, -77.251675; see map AA)

661. Kershaw's Brigade, McLaw's Division, 1st Corps (39.795633, -77.247606; see map AA)

656. McLaw's Division, 1st Corps (39.798474, -77.255914; see map AA)

821. Palmetto Light Artillery (39.786887, -77.254139; see map EE)

177. Pee Dee Artillery (Zimmerman's Battery) (39.820332, -77.246244; see map L)

170. Perrin's Brigade, Pender's Division, 3rd Corps (39.822366, -77.245456; see map L)

VIRGINIA

664. 1st Richmond Howitzers (39.796555, -77.255508; see map AA)

143. 2nd Richmond Howitzers (39.827225, -77.245169; see map H)

145. 2nd Richmond Howitzers (39.826922, -77.244746; see map H)

136. 2nd Rockbridge Artillery (39.828543, -77.244482; see map H)

132. 3rd Richmond Howitzers (39.830818, -77.244368; see map H)

161. Alleghany Artillery (39.827664, -77.213713; see map K)

157. Amherst Virignia Artillery (39.829838, -77.212634; see map K)

651. Ashland Virginia Artillery (39.799587, -77.256051; see map AA)

459. Bedford Virginia Artillery (39.800258, -77.256145; see map U)

439. Blount's Battery (39.805912, -77.256325; see map U)

387. Breathed's Battery, Beckham's Battalion, Cavalry Division (39.837018, -77.168176; see map R)

184. Brockenbrough's Brigade, Heth's Division, 3rd Corps (39.819227, -77.247218; see map L)

422. Brooke's Battery (39.814605, -77.250315; see map U)

73. Charlottsville (Virginia) Battery (39.850661, -77.217077; see map E)

75. Courtney (Virginia) Artillery (39.851282, -77.213373; see map E)

179. Crenshaw's Battery (39.820096, -77.246679; see map L)

133. Dance's Battalion, Early's Division, 2nd Corps (39.83042, -77.2443; see map H)

139. Danville Virginia Artillery (2) (39.827796, -77.244855; see map H)

140. Danville Virginia Artillery (39.827754, -77.244831; see map H)

442. Dearing's Artillery Battalion, Pickett's Division, 1st Corps (39.80511, -77.25619; see map U)

444. Fauquier Artillery (Stribling's Battery) (39.804229, -77.256013; see map U)

155. Fluvanna Virginia Artillery (39.830454, -77.212395; see map K)

183. Fredericksburg Artillery (39.819495, -77.246877; see map L)

427. Garnett's Brigade, Pickett's Division, 1st Corps (39.813524, -77.251254; see map U)

443. Hampden Artillery (39.804822, -77.256045; see map U)

187. Heth's Division, 3rd Corps (39.818635, -77.247713; see map L)

169. Huger Artillery (Moore's Battery) (39.822878, -77.245219; see map L)

391. Jackson's Battery, Cavalry divison (39.834339, -77.170555; see map R)

144. Johnson's Virginia Battery (39.827142, -77.244804; see map H)

141. Johnson's Virginia Battery (39.827474, -77.245238; see map H)

305. Jones Brigade, Johnson's Division, 2nd Corps (39.822382, -77.220154; see map O)

430. Kemper's Brigade, Pickett's Division, 1st Corps (39.812023, -77.25266; see map U)

9. King William Artillery (W. P. Carter's Battery) (39.848814, -77.243859; see map B)

164. Lee Battery (Raines's Battery) (39.826213, -77.213764; see map K)

172. Letcher Artillery (Brander's Battery) (39.821572, -77.245576; see map L)

167. Lewis Artillery (Lewis's Battery) (39.82531, -77.245048; see map L)

419. Mahone's Brigade, Anderson's Division, 3rd Corps (39.81587, -77.249459; see map U)

389. McGregor's Battery, Beckham's Battalion, Cavalry Division (39.835673, -77.169426; see map R)

17. Morris Artillery (Page's Battery) (39.847285, -77.242364; see map B)

171. Norfolk Light Artillery (39.822319, -77.245398; see map L)
14. Orange Artillery (39.848067, -77.24329; see map B)
458. Parker's Battery (39.800818, -77.256259; see map U)
431. Perry's Brigade, Anderson's Division, 3rd Corps (39.811504, -77.252799; see map U)
477. Perry's Brigade, Anderson's Division, 3rd Corps (39.808828, -77.243511; see map V)
420. Poague's Howitzers (39.814583, -77.250557; see map U)
135. Powhattan (Virginia) Artillery (39.829689, -77.244029; see map H)
175. Purcell Artillery (McGraw's Battery) (39.821083, -77.246092; see map L)
441. Richmond Fayette Artillery (39.805328, -77.256143; see map U)
159. Rockbridge Artillery (39.828523, -77.213213; see map K)
165. Salem Artillery (39.82648, -77.244734; see map L)
370. Smith's Brigade, Early's Division, 2nd Corps (39.815222, -77.215817; see map O)
74. Staunton (Virginia) Artillery (39.850762, -77.213468; see map E)
455. Taylor's Battery (39.801249, -77.256212; see map U)
379. Walker's Brigade, Johnson's Division, 2nd Corps (39.816066, -77.215605; see map P)

UNION BATTALIONS

593. Battalion of United States Engineers (39.808084, -77.232614; see map W)

UNION BATTERIES

83. Battery A, 2nd United States Artillery (39.837645, -77.25157; see map G)
121. Battery A, 2nd United States Artillery (39.83197, -77.251164; see map G)
528. Battery A, 4th United States Artillery (39.81306, -77.235879; see map W)
239. Battery B, 1st United States Artillery (39.821229, -77229302; see map N)
631. Batteries B and L, 2nd United States Artillery (39.804751, -77.222464; see map X)
599. Batteries B and L, 2nd United States Artillery (39.807843, -77.230872; see map W)
628. Battery C, 3rd United States Artillery (39.804679, -77.230198; see map W)
579. Battery C, 4th United States Artillery (39.807672, -77.235825; see map W)

565. Battery C, 5th United States Artillery, 1st Regular Artillery, Artillery Reserve (39.810032, -77.235955; see map W)

765. Battery D, 2nd United States Artillery (39.798843, -77.22961; see map CC)

804. Battery D, 5th United States Artillery (Hazlett's Battery) (39.791929, -77.236559; see map CC)

832. Battery E, 4th United States Artiller (39.783168, -77.246358; see map EE)

407. Batteries E and G, 1st United States Artillery (39.821414, -77.164881; see map S)

409. Batteries E and G, 1st United States Artillery (39.819005, -77.168583; see map T)

286. Battery F, United States Artillery (39.816114, -77.234348; see map N)

304. Battery F, United States Artillery (39.813046, -77.223783; see map N)

294. Batteries F and K, 3rd United States Artillery (39.814255, -77.234673; see map N)

485. Batteries F and K, 3rd United States Artillery (39.807644, -77.244581; see map V)

287. Battery G, 2nd United States Artillery (39.816473, -77.234113; see map N)

67. Battery G, 4th United States Artillery (39.845592, -77.226157; see map D)

268. Battery G, 4th United States Artillery (39.819926, -77.230804; see map N)

270. Battery H, 1st United States Artillery (39.819327, -77.231244; see map N)

200. Battery I, 1st United States Artillery (39.816293, -77.234883; see map M)

622. Battery I, 5th United States Artillery (39.802808, -77.237978; see map W)

493. Battery K, 4th United States Infantry (39.80565, -77.246806; see map V)

323. Battery K, 5th United States Artillery (39.820046, -77.220292; see map O)

303. Battery K, 5th United States Artillery (39.812935, -77.223797; see map N)

411. Battery M, 2nd United States Artillery (39.818304, -77.169359; see map T)

UNION REGIMENTS

730. 2nd United States Infantry (39.795555, -77.24117; see map BB)

734. 3rd United States Infantry (39.795218, -77.240781; see map BB)

735. 4th United States Infantry (39.795055, -77.240936; see map BB)

737. 6th United States Infantry (39.794866, -77.241026; see map BB)

741. 7th United States Infantry (39.795076, -77.241329; see map BB)

298. 8th United States Infantry (39.814483, -77.232303; see map N)

742. 10th United States Infantry (39.794898, -77.241436; see map BB)

743. 11th United States Infantry (39.794775, -77.241266; see map BB)

738. 12th United States Infantry (39.794797, -77.241049; see map BB)

746. 14th United States Infantry (39.794026, -77.240815; see map BB)

744. 17th United States Infantry (39.794465, -77.241416; see map BB)

UNION BRIGADES

112. 1st Brigade, 1st Division, 1st Corps (39.83494, -77.250018; see map G)

92. 1st Brigade, 1st Division, 1st Corps (July 1) (39.835308, -77.254559; see map G)

727. 1st Brigade, 1st Division, 2nd Corps (39.796214, -77.241762; see map BB)

500. 1st Brigade, 1st Division, 3rd Corps (39.803789, -77.248298; see map V)

689. 1st Brigade, 1st Division, 5th Corps (39.797173, -77.246294; see map BB)

625. 1st Brigade, 1st Division, 6th Corps headquarters (39.80058, -77.234526; see map W)

245. 1st Brigade, 1st Division, 11th Corps (39.82156, -77.227466; see map N)

360. 1st Brigade, 1st Division, 12th Corps (39.815702, -77.217769; see map O)

35. 1st Brigade, 2nd Division, 1st Corps (39.841473, -77.242858; see map B)

557. 1st Brigade, 2nd Division, 2nd Corps (39.810746, -77.235905; see map W)

486. 1st Brigade, 2nd Division, 3rd Corps (39.807606, -77.24425; see map V)

736. 1st Brigade, 2nd Division, 5th Corps (39.794939, -77.240949; see map BB)

149. 1st Brigade, 2nd Division, 11th Corps (39.835145, -77.227795; see map I)

776. 1st Brigade, 2nd Division, 12th Corps headquarters (39.797638, -77.23444; see map CC)

332. 1st Brigade, 2nd Division, 12th Corps (39.818652, -77.219728; see map O)

404. 1st Brigade, 2nd Division, Cavalry Corps (39.825909, -77.163139; see map S)

122. 1st Brigade, 3rd Division, 1st Corps (39.83166, -77.251225; see map G)

241. 1st Brigade, 3rd Division, 2nd Corps (39.821642, -77.228919; see map N)

725. 1st Brigade, 3rd Division, 5th Corps (39.796458, -77.2409; see map BB)

336. 1st Brigade, 3rd Division, 6th Corps (39.817826, -77.219738; see map O)

44. 1st Brigade, 3rd Division, 11th Corps (39.840748, -77.234924; see map C)

827. 1st Brigade, 3rd Division, Cavalry Corps (39.785661, -77.249057; see map EE)

598. 1st Brigade, Horse Artillery, Cavalry Corps (39.807825, -77.231117; see map W)

580. 1st Regular Brigade, Artillery Reserve, Brigade (39.807653, -77.235872; see map W)

512. 1st Volunteer Brigade, Artillery Reserve (39.800971, -77.248041; see map V)

616. 1st Volunteer Brigade, Artillery Reserve (39.803998, -77.234538; see map W)

39. 2nd Brigade, 1st Division, 1st Corps Headquarters (39.839328, -77.247283; see map B)

692. 2nd Brigade, 1st Division, 2nd Corps (39.797384, -77.24567; see map BB)

752. 2nd Brigade, 1st Division, 3rd Corps (39.793024, -77.242749; see map BB)

704. 2nd Brigade, 1st Division, 5th Corps (39.796016, -77.244052; see map BB)

775. 2nd Brigade, 1st Division, 6th Corps (39.795273, -77.236294; see map CC)

63. 2nd Brigade, 1st Division, 11th Corps (39.845127, -77.227173; see map D)

330. 2nd Brigade, 1st Division, 12th Corps (39.81904, -77.219794; see map O)

4. 2nd Brigade, 1st Division, Cavalry Corps Headquaters (39.844814, -77.247067; see map B)

30. 2nd Brigade, 2nd Division, 1st Corps (39.842624, -77.242411; see map B)

533. 2nd Brigade, 2nd Division, 2nd Corps (39.813083, -77.235431; see map W)

502. 2nd Brigade, 2nd Divison, 3rd Corps (39.802592, -77.246822; see map V)

740. 2nd Brigade, 2nd Division, 5th Corps (39.795145, -77.241462; see map BB)

837. 2nd Brigade, 2nd Division, 6th Corps (39.785092, -77.232687; see map GG)

263. 2nd Brigade, 2nd Division, 11th Corps (39.819941, -77.232948; see map N)

350. 2nd Brigade, 2nd Division, 12th Corps (39.816688, -77.219401; see map O)

590. 2nd Brigade, 2nd Division, Cavalry Corps (39.80826, -77.23459; see map W)

85. 2nd Brigade, 3rd Division, 1st Corps (39.837578, -77.252111; see map G)

217. 2nd Brigade, 3rd Division, 2nd Corps (39.814092, -77.235283; see map M)

784. 2nd Brigade, 3rd Division, 6th Corps (39.796414, -77.234079; see map CC)

60. 2nd Brigade, 3rd Division, 11th Corps (39.843446, -77.22907; see map D)

399. 2nd Brigade, 3rd Division, Cavalry Corps (39.826634, -77.165126; see map S)

408. 2nd Brigade Horse Artillery, Cavalry Corps (39.820347, -77.166496; see map T)

254. 2nd Volunteer Brigade, Artillery Reserve, Army of the Potomac (39.820499, -77.228974; see map N)

696. 3rd Brigade, 1st Division, 2nd Corps (39.797241, -77.24521; see map BB)

702. 3rd Brigade, 1st Division, 3rd Corps (39.7965, -77.244213; see map BB)

810. 3rd Brigade, 1st Division, 5th Corps (39.790967, -77.236564; see map CC)

844. 3rd Brigade, 1st Division, 6th Corps (39.78337, -77.228403; see map GG)

380. 3rd Brigade, 1st Division, 12th Corps (39.813196, -77.215464; see map P)

548. 3rd Brigade, 2nd Division, 2nd Corps (39.811948, -77.235526; see map W)

708. 3rd Brigade, 2nd Division, 3rd Corps (39.795939, -77.245346; see map BB)

801. 3rd Brigade, 2nd Division, 5th Corps (39.792311, -77.236267; see map CC)

645. 3rd Brigade, 2nd Division, 6th Corps (39.807931, -77.210116; see map Z)

334. 3rd Brigade, 2nd Division, 12th Corps (39.818314, -77.219497; see map O)

412. 3rd Brigade, 2nd Division, Cavalry Corps (39.818132, -77.169471; see map T)
571. 3rd Brigade, 3rd Division, 1st Corps (39.809293, -77.236461; see map W)
489. 3rd Brigade, 3rd Division, 2nd Corps commemorative (39.806711, -77.244864; see map V)
207. 3rd Brigade, 3rd Division, 2nd Corps headquarters (39.815264, -77.235256; see map M)
816. 3rd Brigade, 3rd Division, 5th Corps (39.788486, -77.237574; see map CC)
771. 3rd Brigade, 3rd Division, 6th Corps (39.796633, -77.23779; see map CC)
272. 3rd Volunteer Brigade, Artillery Reserve (39.818409, -77.231656; see map N)
715. 4th Brigade, 1st Division, 2nd Corps (39.795124, -77.246946; see map BB)
523. 4th Volunteer Brigade, Artillery Reserve (39.81358, -77.235307; see map W)
531. Artillery Brigade, 2nd Corps (39.813174, -77.235534; see map W)
793. Artillery Brigade, 5th Corps (39.793871, -77.234827; see map CC)
592. Brigade of Engineers, Army of the Potomac (39.808014, -77.232923; see map W)
623. Tompkins's Brigade (39.802091, -77.234224; see map W)

UNION DIVISIONS

108. 1st Division, 1st Corps (39.836832, -77.248775; see map G)
609. 1st Division, 2nd Corps (39.805395, -77.234604; see map W)
464. 1st Division, 3rd Corps (39.801456, -77.250041; see map U)
678. 1st Division, 5th Corps (39.798479, -77.245054; see map BB)
778. 1st Division, 6th Corps headquarters (39.797407, -77.23487; see map CC)
70. 1st Division, 11th Corps (39.844883, -77.226691; see map D)
358. 1st Division, 12th Corps (39.8159, -77.217941; see map O)
111. 1st Division, Cavalry Corps (39.835146, -77.249857; see map G)
29. 2nd Division, 1st Corps (39.842565, -77.241319; see map B)
466. 2nd Division, 3rd Corps (39.801502, -77.249929; see map U)
487. 2nd Division, 3rd Corps (39.807255, -77.244516; see map V)
563. 2nd Division, 2nd Corps (39.810378, -77.235781; see map W)
733. 2nd Division, 5th Corps (39.795259, -77.2398; see map BB)
840. 2nd Division, 5th Corps (39.784128, -77.229865; see map GG)
227. 2nd Division, 11th Corps (39.821762, -77.229914; see map N)
341. 2nd Division, 12th Corps (39.817411, -77.219931; see map O)
403. 2nd Division, Cavalry Corps (39.826071, -77.163482; see map S)

397. 2nd Cavalry Division, Extreme Right Flank Army of the Potomac (39.828542, -77.158063; see map S)

114. 3rd Dvision, 1st Corps (39.834137, -77.250625; see map G)

209. 3rd Division, 2nd Corps headquarters (39.815012, -77.235304; see map M)

732. 3rd Division, 5th Corps (39.795647, -77.238811; see map BB)

624. 3rd Division, 6th Army Corps headquarters (39.800927, -77.234283; see map W)

46. 3rd Division, 11th Corps (39.84093, -77.234435; see map C)

829. 3rd Cavalry Division, Cavalry Corps (39.784625, -77.249605; see map EE)

UNION CORPS

110. 1st Corps headquarters cannon (39.835479, -77.249677; see map G)

594. 1st Corps headquarters cannon (39.807661, -77.231748; see map W)

81. 1st Corps (39.837909, -77.251311; see map G)

584. 2nd Corps headquarters cannon (39.808257, -77.234926; see map W)

215. 2nd Corps (39.814348, -77.235256; see map M)

130. 2nd Corps (39.834075, -77.245002; see map H)

518. 3rd Corps headquarters cannon (39.801867, -77242979; see map V)

465. 3rd Corps (39.801467, -77.24999; see map U)

782. 5th Corps Headquarters cannon (39.79698, -77.234361; see map CC)

797. 5th Corps (39.793388, -77.235248; see map CC)

777. 6th Corps Headquarters cannon (39.797509, -77.234774; see map CC)

627. 6th Corps Headquarters (39.799908, -77.234368; see map W)

242. 11th Corps headquarters (39.821518, -77.228891; see map N)

54. 11th Corps (39.842948, -77.231866; see map C)

642. 11th Corps Medical Corps Field Hospitals (39.801129, -77.218194; see map Y)

635. 12th Corps headquarters cannon (39.808093, -77.217893; see map Y)

352. 12th Corps (39.816324, -77.218947; see map O)

585. Cavalry Corps (39.80814, -77.234894; see map W)

ARMY OF THE POTOMAC

77. Army of the Potomac Field Hospital (39.841527, -77.205854; see map F)

297. Army of the Potomac Headquarters (39.814446, -77.232246; see map N)

238. Army of the Potomac (39.82138, -77.22955; see map N)

532. Army of the Potomac (39.81321, -77.235427; see map W)

601. Artillery Reserve, Army of the Potomac (39.807619, -77.230588; see map W)

647. Right Flank of the Infantry of the Army of the Potomac (39.808086, -77.208011; see map Z)

CONFEDERATE BATTALIONS

457. Alexander's Artillery Battalion, 1st Corps (39.800945, -77.256235; see map U)

663. Cabell's Battalion, McLaw's Division, 1st Corps (39.797086, -77.255424; see map AA)

16. Carter's Battalion (39.847888, -77.242961; see map B)

168. Garnett's Artillery Battalion, Heth's Division, 3rd Corps (39.824269, -77.245116; see map L)

677. Henry's Artillery Battalion, Hood's Division, 1st Corps (39.78795, -77.253935; see map AA)

72. Jones's Artillery Battalion, Early's Division, 2nd Corp (39.850667, -77.217963; see map E)

162. Latimer's Battalion, Johnson's Division, 2nd Corps (39.827225, -77.21388; see map K)

138. McIntosh's Artillery Battalion, Artillery Reserve, 3rd Corps (39.827949, -77.244752; see map H)

156. Nelson's Battalion, Artillery Reserve, 2nd Corps (39.829861, -77.212653; see map K)

178. Pegram's Battalion, Artillery Reserve, 3rd Corps (39.820236, -77.246498; see map L)

417. Poague's Battalion, Heth's Division, 3rd Corps (39.816958, -77.248623; see map U)

CONFEDERATE BATTERIES

452. Miller's Battery (39.802699, -72.256073; see map U)

CONFEDERATE BRIGADES

668. Anderson's Brigade, Hood's Division, 1stCorps (39.792469, -77.254988; see map AA)

750. Anderson's Brigade, Hood's Division, 1st Corps (39.793549, -77.245642; see map BB)

93. Archer's Brigade (39.834838, -77.254703; see map G)

418. Archer's Brigade, Heth's Division, 3rd Corps (39.816925, -77.248799; see map U)

429. Armistead's Brigde, Pickett's Division, 1st Corps (39.81267, -77.25199; see map U)

256. Artillery Brigade, 1st Corps (39.821166, -77.228929; see map N)

467. Artillery Brigade, 3rd Corps (39.801528, -77.249854; see map U)

501. Artillery Brigade, 3rd Corps (39.802846, -77.246829; see map V)

50. Artillery Brigade, 11th Corps (39.842187, -77.23374; see map C)

376. Artillery Brigade, 12th Corps (39.813432, -77.222789; see map O)

675. Benning's Brigade, Hood's Division, 1st Corps (39.789277, -77.254116; see map AA)

757. Benning's Brigade, Hood's Division, 1st Corps (39.791309, -77.24356; see map BB)

392. Chambliss' Brigade, Cavalry Division (39.833583, -77.17209; see map R)

100. Davis's Brigade (39.838333, -77.247893; see map G)

190. Davis's Brigade, Heth's Division, 3rd Corps (39.818409, -77.247965; see map L)

53. Doyle's Brigade, Rodes' Division, 2nd Corps (39.842923, -77.232201; see map C)

385. Fitzhugh Lee's Brigade, Cavalry Division (39.838315, -77.166908; see map R)

71. Gordon's Brigade, Early's Division, 2nd Corps (39.84493, -77.226496; see map D)

388. Hampton's Brigade, Cavalry Division (39.836373, -77.168824; see map R)

125. Imboden's Brigade (Cavalry) (39.827305, -77.252903; see map G)

394. Jenkins' Brigade, Cavalry Division (39.832439, -77.17393; see map R)

127. Jones's Brigade (Cavalry) (39.827144, -77.253031; see map G)

176. Lane's Brigade, Pender's Division, 3rd Corps (39.820613, -77.246221; see map L)

126. Robertson's Brigade (Cavalry) (39.827241, -77.252929; see map G)

755. Robertson's Brigade, Hood's Division, 1st Corps (39.792169, -77.242747; see map BB)

670. Robertson's Brigade, Hood's Division, 1st Corps (39.79047, -77.254439; see map AA)

180. Scales' Brigade, Pender's Division, 3rd Corps (39.819822, -77.246816; see map L)

377. Steuart's Brigade, Johnson's Division, 2nd Corps (39.817276, -77.21523; see map P)

174. Thomas's Brigade, Pender's Division, 3rd Corps (39.821261, -77.246124; see map L)

CONFEDERATE DIVISIONS

433. Anderson's Division, 3rd Corps (39.809649, -77.254437; see map U)

386. Beckham's Horse Artillery, Cavalry Division (39.837331, -77.167941; see map R)

390. Cavalry Division (39.834977, -77.170084; see map R)

673. Hood's Division (39.790131, -77.25433; see map AA)

307. Johnson's Division, 2nd Corps (39.820532, -77.216764; see map O)

652. McLaw's Division, 1st Corps (39.799267, -77.256129; see map AA)

173. Pender's Division, 3rd Corps (39.821552, -77.245754; see map L)

428. Pickett's Division, 1st Corps (39.813174, -77.251517; see map U)

13. Rodes's Division (39.84839, -77.243326; see map B)

CONFEDERATE CORPS

456. 1st Corps Army of Northern Virginia (39.801108, -77.256244; see map U)

7. 2nd Corps, Army of Northern Virginia Headquarters (39.847671, -77.245358; see map B)

152. 2nd Corps, Army of Northern Virginia headquarters (39.829098, -77.226561; see map J)

181. 3rd Corps, Army of Northern Virigina (39.819814, -77.246913; see map L)

191. 3rd Corps headquarters cannon (39.818069, -77.248166; see map L)

648. Longstreet's (1st Corps) headquarters cannon (39.800191, -77.25628; see map AA)

ARMY OF NORTHERN VIRGINIA

128. Army of Northern Virginia Headquarters cannon (39.834782, -77.245493; see map H)

425. Army of Northern Virginia (39.814163, -77.250596; see map U)

142. Army of Northern Virginia s (39.827326, -77.244892; see map H)

OTHER

195. Bliss Farm site (39.816993, -77.241637; see map M)
204. Brian Barn and House (39.815506, -77.235251; see map M)
474. Codori House (39.811335, -77.2402; see map V)
252. Evergreen Cemetery Gatehouse (39.820772, -77.229347; see map N)
278. Gettysburg National Military Park (39.817024, -77.234556; see map N)
595. Hummelbaugh Farm (39.807726, -77.231659; see map W)
414. J. Spangler Farm (39.817852, -77.16935; see map T)
491. Klingle Farm (39.806283, -77.246243; see map V)
406. Lott Farm (39.822868, -77.162409; see map S)
86. McPherson Barn (39.836882, -77.251603; see map G)
826. Right Flank of the Army of Northern Virginia (39.784329, -77.252159; see map EE)
660. Rose Farm (39.797168, -77.24966; see map AA)
393. Rummel farm (39.833609, -77.171695; see map R)
497. Sherfy Farm (39.803669, -77.248996; see map V)
761. Slyder Farm (39.788898, -77.246727; see map BB)
666. Snyder Farm (39.792719, -77.254632; see map AA)
517. Trostle Barn (39.802436, -77.212825; see map Y)
301. Widow Leister House (39.814634, -77.232096; see map N)

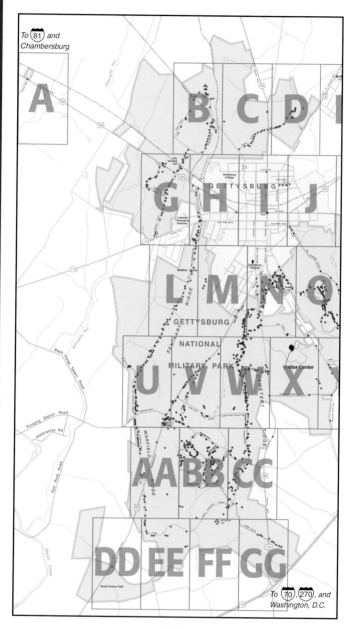

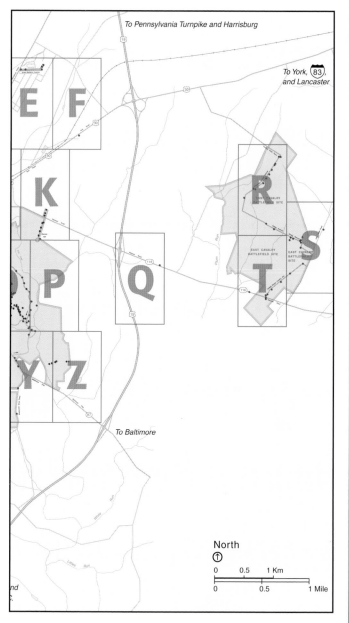

To Pennsylvania Turnpike and Harrisburg

To York, 83, and Lancaster

E F

K

R
EAST CAVALRY
BATTLEFIELD SITE

S

EAST CAVALRY
BATTLEFIELD SITE

EAST CAVALRY
BATTLEFIELD SITE

O P Q

T

Y Z

To Baltimore

North

0   0.5   1 Km

0   0.5   1 Mile

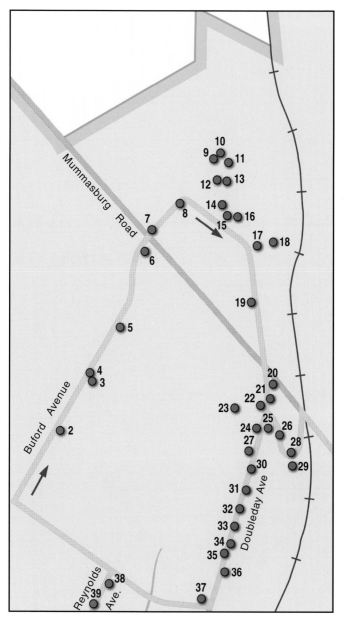

MAP C

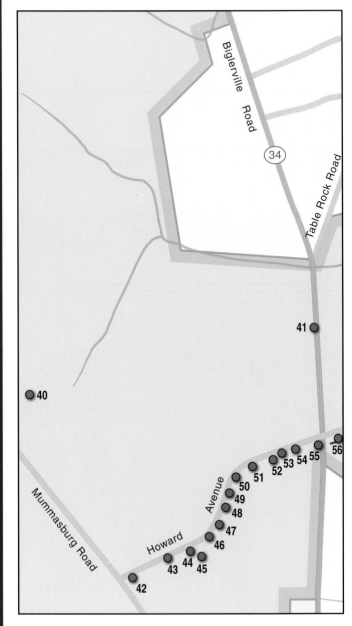

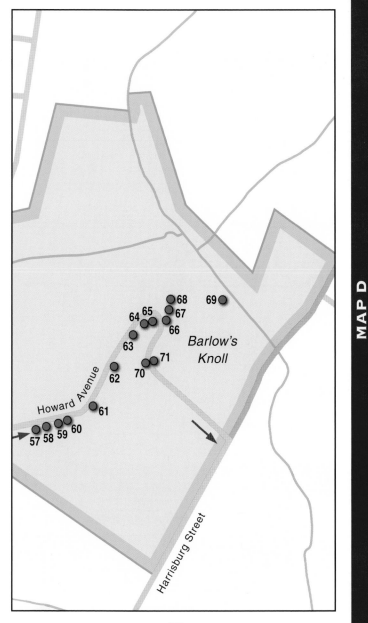

57 58 59 60 61 62 63 64 65 66 67 68 69 70 71

Howard Avenue

Barlow's Knoll

Harrisburg Street

199

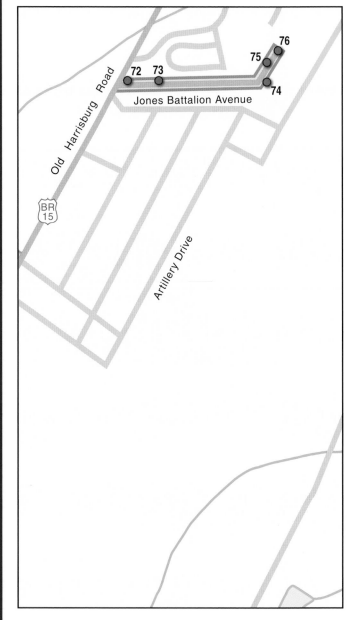

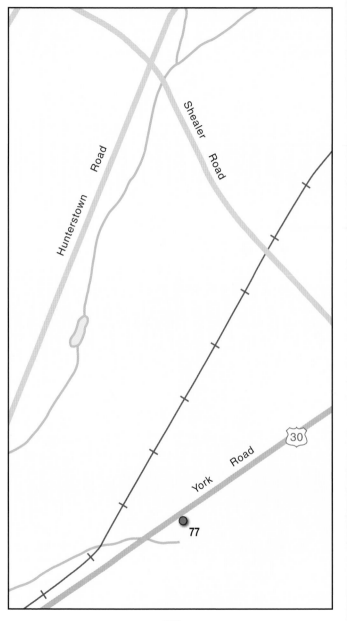

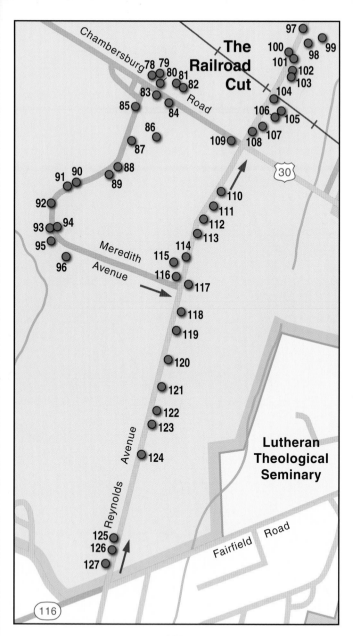

The
The Railroad Cut

Chambersburg

97
100
101
99
98
102
103
104
106
105
107
108
109

78 79
80 81
82
Road
83
85
84
86
87
88
89
90
91
92
93 94
95
96

Meredith

Avenue

110
111
112
113
114
115
116
117
118
119
120
121
122
123
124

Avenue

Reynolds

125
126
127

30

Lutheran
Theological
Seminary

Fairfield Road

116

202

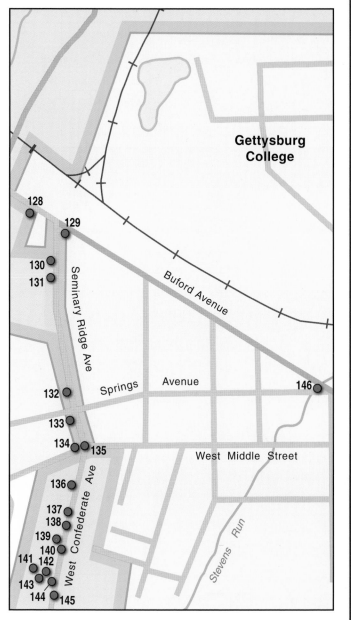

Gettysburg College

128

129

130

131

Seminary Ridge Ave

Buford Avenue

Springs Avenue

146

132

133

134 135

West Middle Street

136

137

138

139

140

141 142

143

144 145

West Confederate Ave

Stevens Run

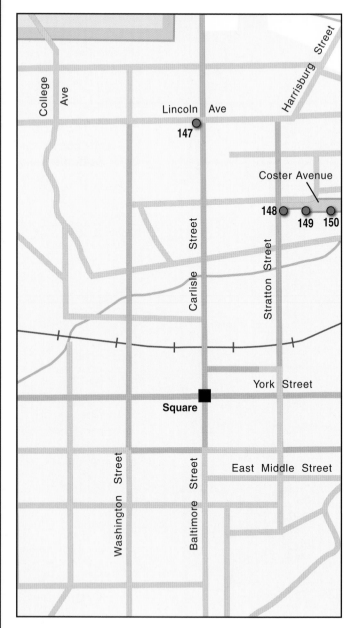

MAP I

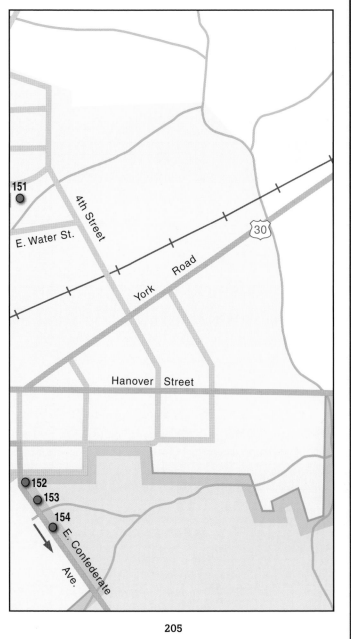

205

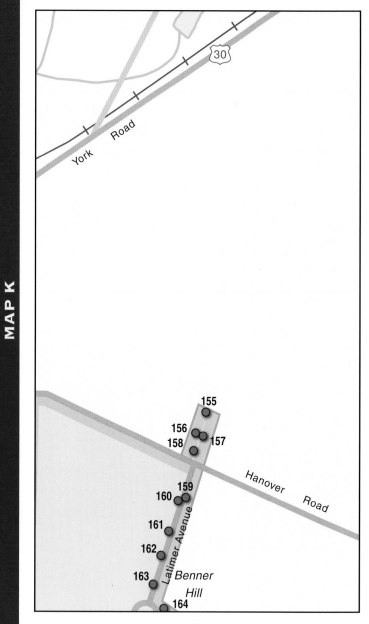

155

156
158 157

Hanover Road

159
160

161

162

Latimer Avenue

163 Benner

Hill

164

York Road

30

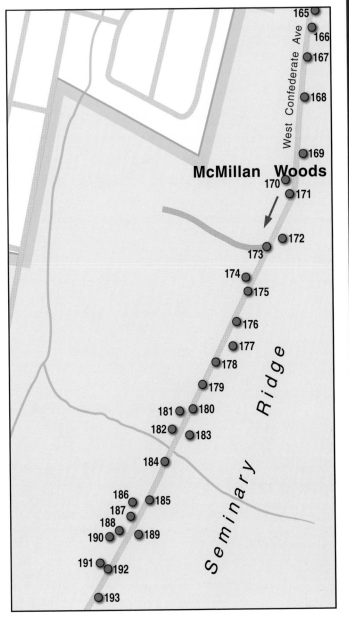

165

166

167

168

West Confederate Ave

169

McMillan Woods

170

171

172

173

174

175

176

177

178

179

181 180

182 183

184

186 185

187

188

190 189

191 192

193

Seminary Ridge

MAP L

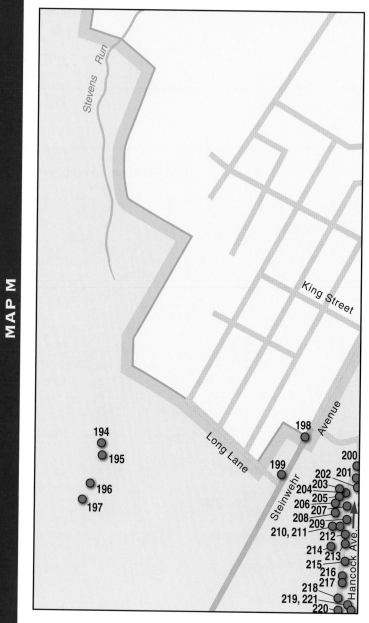

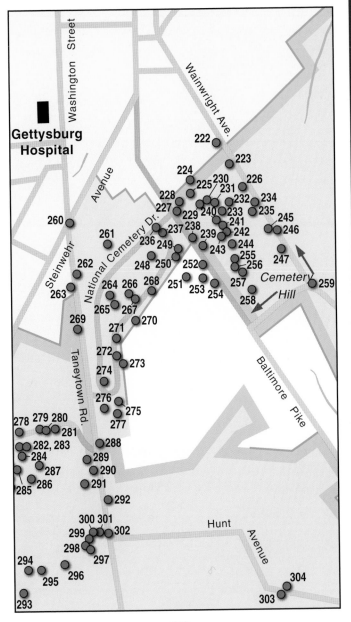

MAP N

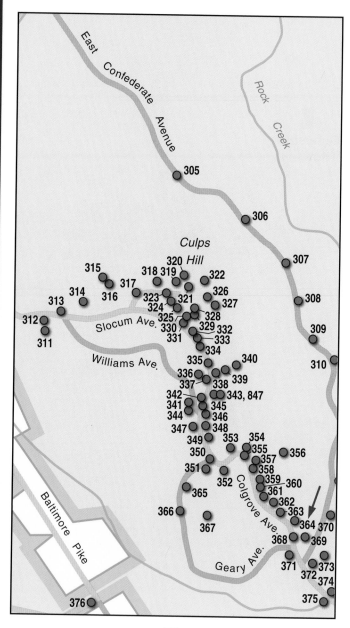

East Confederate Avenue

Rock Creek

305

306

307

Culps Hill

320
318 319
315
317
313 314 316 323
312 311

322
326
327
321
324
325
328
308

Slocum Ave.
330
329 332
331
333
334
309

310

Williams Ave.
335 340

336 338 339

337
343, 847

342
341
345
344
346
347
348

349 353 354

350 355
351 357
358
352 359 360
365 361

362
366 363
367 364 370

368 369

Colgrove Ave.

Baltimore Pike

Geary Ave.
371 373
372 374

376 375

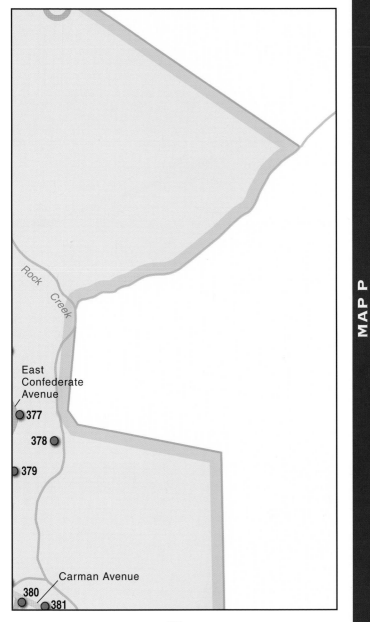

Rock Creek

East
Confederate
Avenue

○ 377

378 ○

○ 379

Carman Avenue

380
○   ○ 381

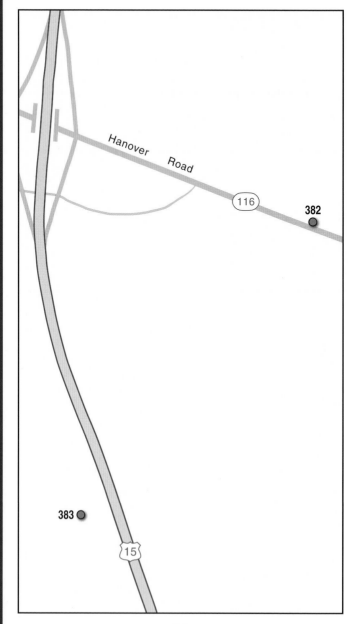

Hanover Road

116

382

383

15

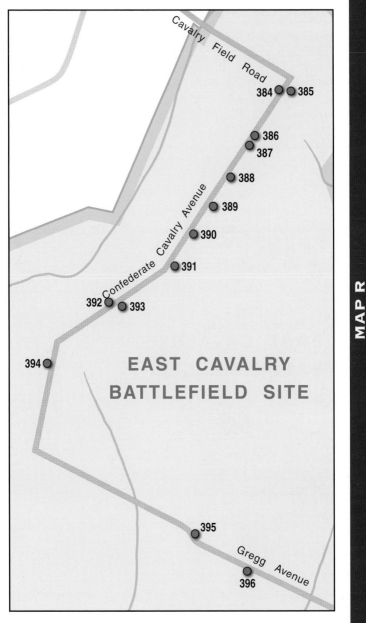

Cavalry Field Road

384 385

386
387

388

Confederate Cavalry Avenue

389

390

391

392 393

394

EAST CAVALRY
BATTLEFIELD SITE

395

Gregg Avenue

396

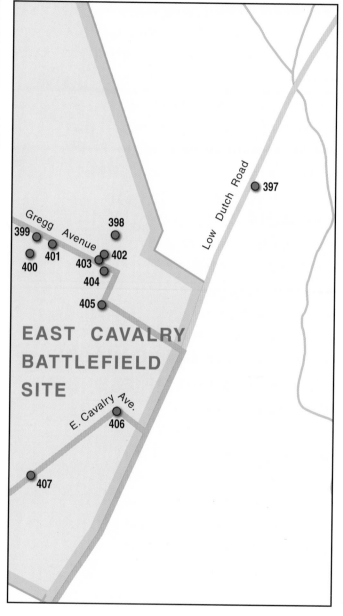

MAP S

Low Dutch Road

● 397

Gregg Avenue

399 ●   ● 398
● ● 401   ● 402
400   ● 403
● 404

● 405

EAST CAVALRY
BATTLEFIELD
SITE

E. Cavalry Ave.
● 406

● 407

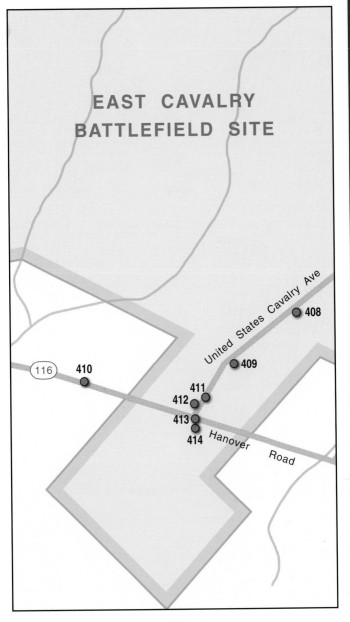

EAST CAVALRY
BATTLEFIELD SITE

116   410

United States Cavalry Ave

408

409

411

412

413

414   Hanover   Road

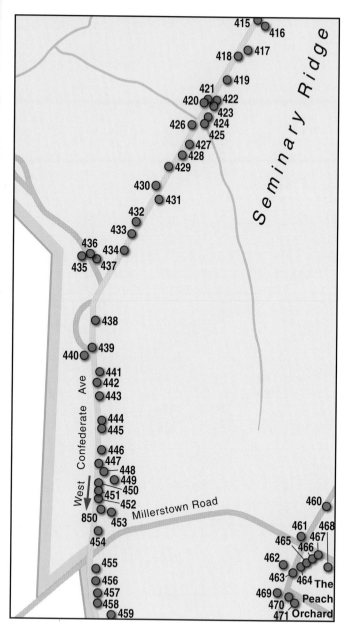

Seminary Ridge

415
416
418
417
419
421
420
422
423
426
424
425
427
428
429
430
431
432
433
436
434
435
437
438
439
440
441
442
443
444
445
446
447
448
449
450
451
452
850
453
454
455
456
457
458
459

West   Confederate   Ave

Millerstown Road

460
461
468
467
465
466
462
463
464
The
469
470
Peach
471
Orchard

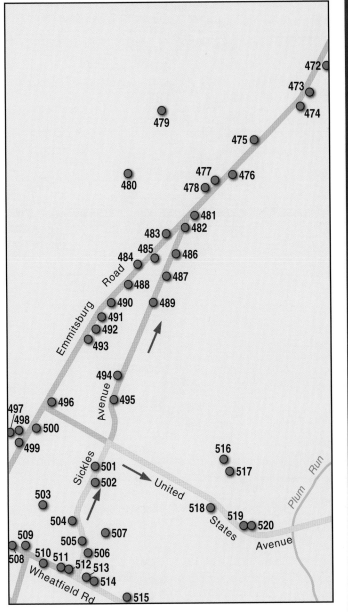

MAP V

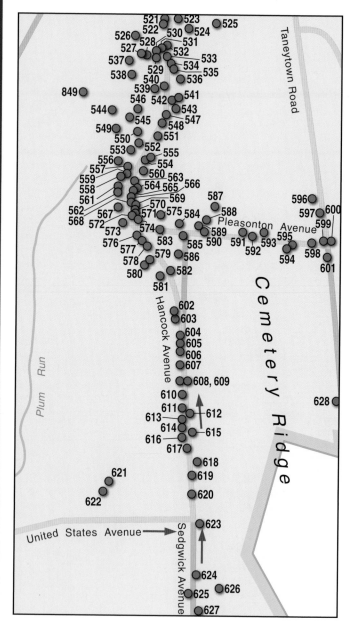

Taneytown Road

Cemetery Ridge

Plum Run

Hancock Avenue

Pleasonton Avenue

United States Avenue

Sedgwick Avenue

521
522
523
524
525
526
527
528
530
531
532
533
534
535
536
537
529
538
540
539
546
542
541
543
849
544
545
547
548
549
550
551
552
553
555
556
554
557
560
563
559
564
565
566
558
561
569
562
570
587
567
571
575
584
588
568
572
574
589
573
576
583
585
590
591
593
595
577
579
586
592
594
598
578
582
601
580
581
596
597
600
599
628
602
603
604
605
606
607
608, 609
610
611
612
613
614
615
616
617
618
619
620
621
622
623
624
625
626
627

218

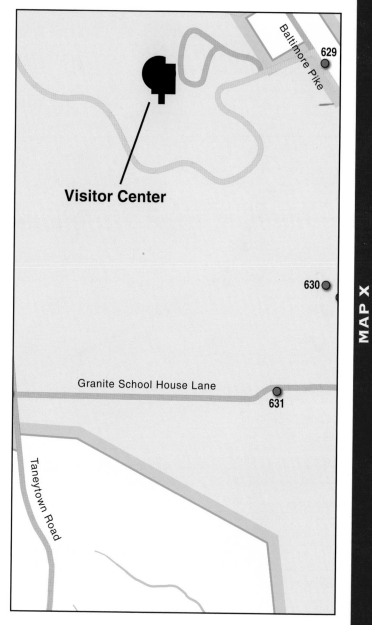

Visitor Center

Baltimore Pike

629

630

631

Granite School House Lane

Taneytown Road

MAP X

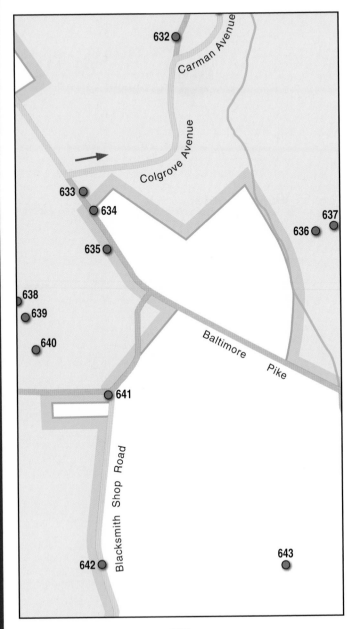

MAP Y

632

Carman Avenue

Colgrove Avenue

633
634

635

636 637

638
639

640

Baltimore Pike

641

Blacksmith Shop Road

643

642

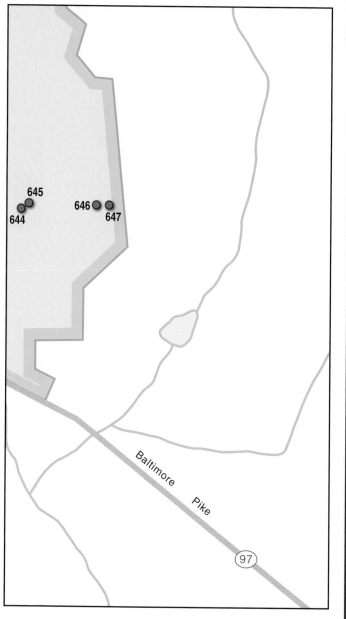

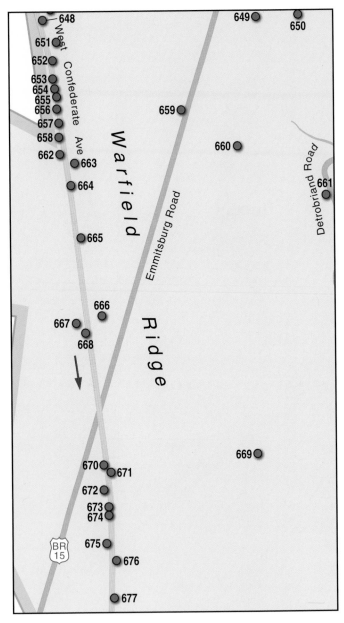

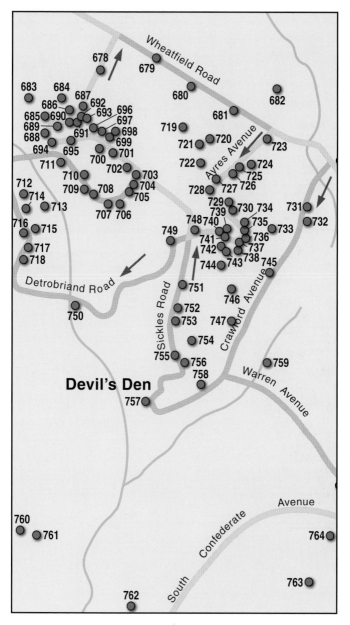

Wheatfield Road

678
679

683 684
687
686 692
685 690 693 696
689 697
688 691 698
694 695 699
711 700 701
712 710 702 703
714 709 708 704
713 707 706 705
716 715
717
718

680
682
681
719
721 720 723
722 Ayres Avenue 724
728 727 725 726
729 730 734 731
739 735 732
748 740 736 733
749 741 742 737 738
744 743 745

Detrobriand Road

750

Sickles Road
751
752
753
746
747
754
755 756 Crawford Avenue 759
758 Warren Avenue

Devil's Den

757

760
761

764

763

762 South Confederate Avenue

223

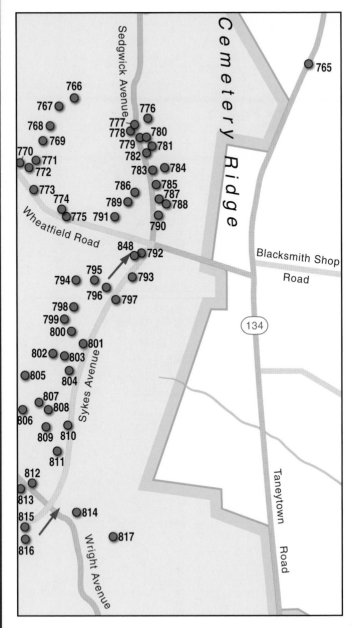

MAP CC

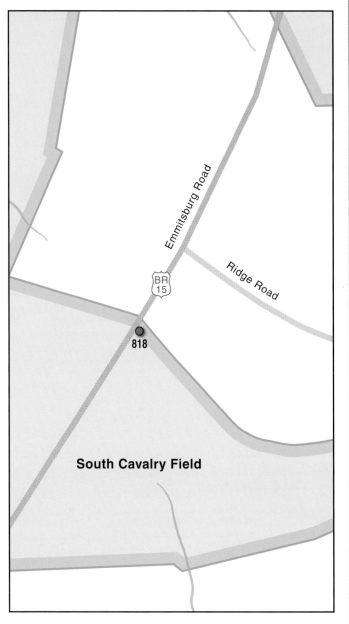

South Cavalry Field

Emmitsburg Road

Ridge Road

BR 15

818

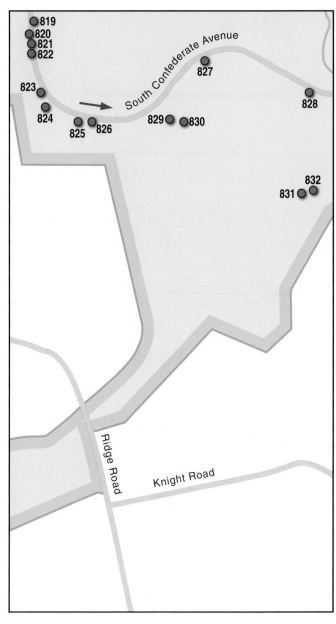

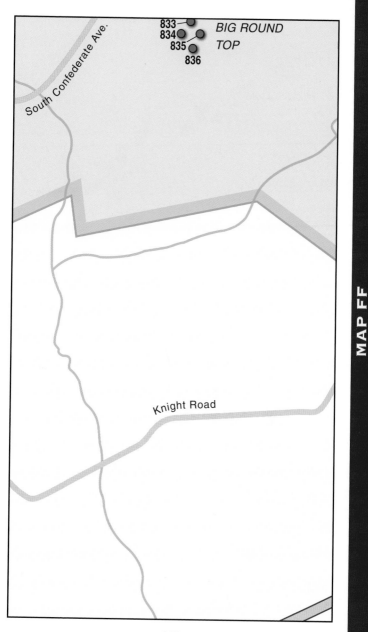

833
834
835
836

BIG ROUND TOP

South Confederate Ave.

Knight Road

MAP FF

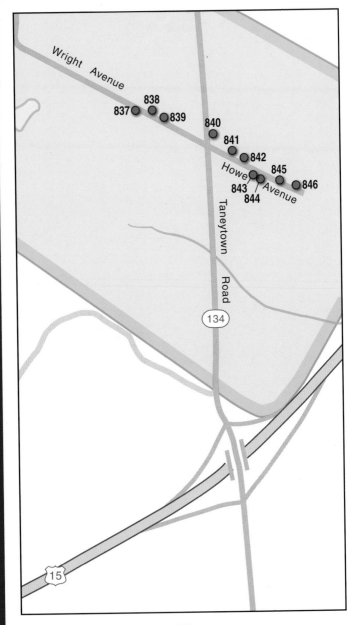